Belongings

Also by Margaret Hasse

Books

Stars Above, Stars Below
In a Sheep's Eye, Darling
Milk and Tides
Earth's Appetite
Between Us
Summoned

Chapbooks

Shelter (in collaboration with artist Sharon DeMark)
The Call of Glacier Park

Anthologies

A Little Book of Abundance (Editor)
Rocked by the Waters (Co-editor with Athena Kildegaard)

Belongings

new and selected poems

Margaret Hasse

Nodin Press

ISBN: 978-1-947237-63-6

Library of Congress Control Number: 2024945530

Book design: John Toren
Set in Galliard type

Published by
Nodin Press
210 Edge Place
Minneapolis, MN 55418
www.nodinpress.com

Printed in the United States

There is no house
like the house of belonging.

David Whyte

Contents

from **Milk and Tides** ▪ 2008

from **Earth's Appetite** ▪ 2013

Introduction

A NEW AND SELECTED book of poems often reveals the subjects a poet has stayed with for many years. In fact, not just "stayed with," but become obsessed by, guarded, nurtured, and grown ever more deeply in debt to. In the case of Margaret Hasse's *Belongings*, this period stretches from 1984 to 2024.

From her very first book, *Stars Above, Stars Below*, Hasse stakes out what matters to her. And thus the title of her new and selected: *Belongings*. The central question is not what belongs to her, but what and who does she belong to, beginning with family. Over decades, what "family" constitutes shifts and develops in the poems: from parents and siblings, to husband and children and the larger sense of family represented by connections with friends, pets, gardens, the earth itself. Indeed, to the "stars above and stars below."

At the heart of what attracts me to Hasse's poetry is the need to explore, to belong to new and different realities. "Grace to be born/and live as variously as possible," Frank O'Hara wrote. I see this quality all through Hasse's poems. It is possible that what she belongs to most deeply is not a particular place or person but to this spirited living variously.

In Hasse's poems, written over many years, living variously guides her again and again into being whatever she is meant to be at that particular moment in her life: whether worrying about and loving a child, grieving a death, celebrating the joy she takes in a particular landscape, her restlessness—which is really a kind of openness—leads her to discover the glory of being whatever one is "meant to be," as she puts it in "A Garden of Her Own," a poem for a beloved friend:

How appealing she is in her greening growth.
What she touches becomes fruitful,
more tasty, more beautiful—
it becomes whatever it meant to be.

These poems are maps for all of us to follow in our own efforts to become, even if only momentarily, who we are meant to be. At such moments, her poems frequently leave in their wake a feeling of peace for the reader, a hard-earned resolution, even if the resolution is temporary.

There are so many kinds of belonging in this book! An early poem called "High School Boyfriend" concludes:

In the dark lovers' lanes
you touched my face
and found me there.

The feeling of being found—by people, by landscape, by animals, by the troubled world—is what belonging is all about in Hasse's poems.

A particularly revelatory discovery appears in poems about living in a culture often divided against itself. This comes out most frequently in poems inspired by the experience of parenting Black sons who have no choice but to live the culture's racism on their skins. As Hasse writes:

He's a brown man on foot in a city troubled
by recent deaths at the hands of men in blue;

what is life for but to trouble
oneself to care for loved ones in good times
and through their troubles.

In "One Woman Telling," a wonderful sequence from *In a Sheep's Eye, Darling*, Hasse's second book, "telling" has very much to do with being a woman learning what her life is meant to be; where being open to the world carries her.

A poem called "Exit Alone" ends this way:

Solitude is like bursting out of a house
where we are warm and loved, but sleepy.
Outdoors is sharp blue.
Its smells slap me awake: catalpa, wet dirt,
the yeasty odor of grain mills,
the old dark blast of trains.

For Hasse, solitude is a gift that she seeks out, and finds, again and again. Perhaps solitude is the ultimate place of belonging for her or at least for her consciousness as a poet. It does indeed slap her awake so that the senses become sharpened and blazingly alive. She belongs to the "yeasty odor" of the grain mills and to the sound of "the old dark blast of trains," a truly wonderful line of poetry.

If solitude is a gateway to belonging, sensuality is yet another, as in this small poem about belonging to one's body and helping another belong to their body.

Giving a Massage

Here, the archipelago down your spine,
here, the dolphin dip of your lower back,

here, the firm reefs of your ribs,
here, the coral in your breasts,
here, the small shells on your fingertips,
here, the shoals near your temples,
here, the deep current of your mouth . . .

Although many of Hasse's poems are narrative, there are also often moments of great lyric intensity, sudden realizations that approach the whole subject of "belongings" in an entirely different way than the more patient art of narrative. In her work, moments of sudden realization feel like little Zen koans. They are also gifts, the kinds of gifts that only come because the poet has made a lifelong practice of paying attention, not only to the world inside her and her own past, but also to the world around her.

As I read the new poems, and then the poems from earlier books, I realized that what holds all these poems together—a theme that develops as the decades pass—is the attention of love over time: what its cost is, what pleasures it brings with it, what makes it possible. Here is the wonderful concluding stanza of a recent love poem, "Without":

In a hospital
windows stay sealed.
It's been five days.
You must get better.
You must return
to share our bed,
hear birds stir
in the morning,
say my breath
reminds you
of damp leaves.

The urgency of the lines "You must getter better./ You must return" is heartbreaking. The way that the poet's breath reminds her beloved of "damp leaves"—so unexpected an image, precise and intimate—gives the poem remarkable authority and presence.

Perhaps this is as good a place as any to end this essay. I must quit quoting poems and let you get to the poems on your own. I will just add that this is a wonderful book to read straight through, from the earliest poems to the new ones. It's lovely to move more and more deeply into Hasse's work, her voice, her openness and sense of belonging, which is at once sacred and profane.

– Jim Moore
Minneapolis, 2024

Jim Moore has lived and been writing poetry in Minnesota's Twin Cities for more than four decades. He's been a generous friend and mentor to many writers, including Margaret. In 1975 Jim introduced her, a new poet, at a Loft Literary Center event. Jim has published seven poetry collections, including *Prognosis* (Graywolf Press, 2021.) He's won many awards for his poetry and received grants from the Bush Foundation, the Minnesota State Arts Board, the Loft-McKnight and the Guggenheim Foundation. Jim's poems have appeared in numerous anthologies and magazines, including *The New Yorker, The Paris Review,* and *The Nation*. He lives in Minneapolis and Spoleto, Italy, with his wife the photographer JoAnn Verburg.

Belongings

Stars Above, Stars Below

1984

Being Still

She's a quiet clapper in the bell of the prairie,
a girl who likes to be alone.
Today she's hiked four miles down
ravines' low cool blueness.

Bending under a barbed wire, she's in
grass fields at the edge of the Great Plains.
Wise to openness, she finds it a familiar place.
Her clothes swell like wheat bread.

When she returns to her parents' house
the foxtails and burrs have come home, too.
The plants seem intent on living in new ground.
She's the carrier. Carrier is a precision
learned in summer's biology class.
She likes to think of ripening seeds,
a cargo inside the bellies of flying birds—
birds like red-winged blackbirds that skim
the air and land, alert on their cattail stalks.
They allow her a silent manner.
They go about their red-winged business
of crying to each other, dipping their beaks
into the swampy stand of ditch water
full of the phantom of green.

The stiller she is the more everything moves
in the immense vocabulary of being.

Light in the Head

At thirteen she begins having fainting spells.
All indoor places are suspect,
especially churches.
The voice of the minister calls a blush
to her pale arms.
He's reading from Saint Paul, and badly.

Her imperturbable mother tongues
the back sides of her teeth.
She knows the signs.
She is glad for an excuse to remember
how sparks once flew
from the touch of everything.

Morning, and the world looks brand-new
as if all its windows had been washed.
The girl rises
and steps into her body.
She has decided to wear it
for the rest of her life.

My Mother's Lullaby

When my mother
smelling of milk and bread
brushes the long robe of my hair,
the vines spring roses.
We wake in a white bed
floating with feather pillows.
Morning patterns her face.
She curls me in her arms;
she is a seashell,
white and full of song.

And now I come to tuck
my little mother into bed.
I am too young to be empty-armed
and the weeds in my throat
will not let me sing lullabies.

Waiting has teeth in it.

My mother smiles at me
and wraps around herself.
I won't see her cry;
her wheat body does not even shake.
She will not know
how the echoes return.
Silent tears are turquoise
peacock feathers that tickle
and the hyena in me laughs,
crazy, crazy,

and my mother
on her thin shelved bed
hears the dogs move restlessly,
the clack of their nails on linoleum.
She knows they have come for her.
She whimpers, they whimper.

Soon there will be no one
to tell me what I was like
when I was a child.

Trying to Save Ourselves

We girls are in the swimming pool
in September after they've pulled the plug.
Now the only blue is paint
loose in large patches like eczema,
and Craig Kaiser is calling my name
from over in the deep end.

Boys' soft tongues, hard hands
begged us to let go, and our bodies
wanted to shout back, swim in over our heads.
But in 1965 the campaign on the side
of not letting go was tremendous.

Our mothers enlisted their large words
speaking of menstruation and marital bonds,
of brassieres worn like life jackets,
making all things more formal
so that they belonged not to us
but to those small town hens
who cackled over our virginity.

In school the film for girls only
confirmed our bodies would condemn us,
our sins balloon and live forever.
Born out of control, the unwanted ghost:
a face lost to the family album.
Some of the boys learned this too,
peeking through slices of light
that fell into the black room where we sat,
hot packages under wraps.

They Leave You Lonely

Daniel wanted my friend Patricia,
who wasn't a pompom girl,
but wore her skirts short anyway.
Over cherry Cokes served in tulip glasses,
we decided that upperclassmen
leave you lonely.
But when he called
to ask her to be his date
at the homecoming prom,
her answer was an eager *Yes.*

That Friday we won the big game,
and Daniel danced close to Patricia,
braiding his arms around her.
Her black dress-up dress
cupped her seat with satin.
Moon River crooned out
of the record player as glitter
began to flake from the streamers
above the gym floor, falling
like silver dust on the couples below.

They drove the borrowed car
directly into the country,
parking west of town.
October's cool edge kept
the heater running.
Their mouths spun candied
webs of moisture.
The huge hulk of the Chevrolet

held their damp and yearning bodies,
darkness within darkness.
While exhaust poured blue
beyond the back seat,
stars fell slowly out of the sky.
And in the early morning
the motor stopped running.

Downtown Saturday noon
Connie Sorenson whispered
that they found them—
still, embracing.
They say it doesn't hurt
and that you never know
it's not air you're breathing.

High School Boyfriend

You are hometown.
You are all my favorite places
the last summer I grew up.
Every once in a while
I write you
in my head
to ask how Vietnam
and a big name college
came between us.
We tried to stay in touch
through the long distance
hum and fleck of phone calls.

It was inevitable
that I should return
to the small prairie town
and find you
pumping gas, driving a truck, measuring lumber,
and we'd exchange
weather talk,
never able to break through words
and time to say simply:
Are you as happy
as I wanted you to be?

And still I'm stirred
by musky cigarette smoke
on a man's brown suede jacket.
Never having admitted the tenderness
of your hands, I feel them now

through my skin.
Parking on breezy nights,
in cars, floating passageways,
we are tongue and tongue like warm cucumbers.

I would walk backward
along far country roads
through late evenings cool as moving water,
heavy as red beer,
to climb into that August.

In the dark lovers' lanes
you touched my face
and found me there.

Incident

We found her on our side stoop
like a stray animal, wincing
under the attention of our car lights.
While we waited for action
to occur to us, she assembled
her confusion slightly
and vanished down the road
toward the railroad tracks
where I've seen people
wrapped in leaves, sleeping.

The moon carved
the backyard into pieces.
We walked to the edge of the lilac,
looked up to the stars, each one
polished and well-placed.
Except the ones whose fall
announced their failing beauty
with a brief white scar.

A Notch in the Spiral

We've returned to autumn
leaving summer a clear lake on which lilies float.
We are back from the season of light,
of lying in warm grass and watching clouds fly.
We're back from a time of round birds,
flagrantly yellow.

Summer still remains in my hair.
Hands sometimes hold sleek water.
There is the sweet cider of apples in store
and two combs of honey on the shelf.

Now apples on the tree are faces,
the porch light is out,
and we huddle behind our separate doors.

We come back to autumn,
to zucchini that wilt like witches' shoes,
to games of solitaire at night,
to silence in the wake of snow geese
that pass high overhead
and empty our mouths with their cries.

after a theme of Seferis

Lacking Ambition

The little lively sparrows light
like a swirl of leaves on the patio.
They are desperately busy
with their daily requirements of food
one-quarter of their weight.
The birds are all pulse and feathers.
They make me tired.

The story of *The Little Engine That Could*
is being read in the next room.
It makes me tired—
all the huffing and puffing.
What we need is to be able
to give up more.
To lay our hands in our laps,
that still of pure absorption,
falling for the world in a way
that we may sit for hours
eyeing things softly
in the delicate manner of light.

Countertops, tables,
books observed as things
apart from their usefulness to us.
In appreciating the geranium
I see green, I see red.
I notice dried blossoms but leave them.
They are like dust in my room,
disheveled papers, unanswered letters,
unwashed cups: they are history
not to be tinkered with today.

Exit Alone

Exiting from a movie theater at 8 p.m.
I stand in front of sheer panes of glass.
Orange tongues of clouds loll on the horizon.
The revelation of orange, of eating, drinking
and going to a film alone: certain colors
are seen only when a person is alone.

I'm all alone walking on a city street
regardless that a man in a VW honks
or a window shade goes down in an apartment
or right in front of me a boy falls off his bike
and like most people who fall pretends he didn't
or that he meant to, all along.

Solitude is like bursting out of a house
where we are warm and loved, but sleepy.
Outdoors is sharp blue.
Its smells slap me awake: catalpa, wet dirt,
the yeasty odor of grain mills,
the old dark blast of trains.

In Shape

We throw snowballs
as an early practice for the team.
Turned thirty, it is more difficult
this year to find my way back
to summery demands.
Winter pounds have been added
like a rippling sealskin coat
groomed late at night:
popcorn buttered yellow
and salted apples,
cake for anyone's birthday,
cookies made because
the house seemed cold.

I'm past the time when power
can be purchased as lipstick
or small bikinis, when the chatter
of supermarket magazines
can draw me in
with their proclamations
of the weeks remaining until
swimming suits.
They sell another diet
guaranteed to let me get light.

I toss a chocolate bar
into the silver basket like a score.
I have weight.
I can throw it around.

Night Game at Parade Stadium

You bump into a friend in the bleachers.
He's walked out on a bad movie
to sit in this second-rate field
watching the P.O. men beat the Finks,
a police team. It's that kind of night.

Professional ball players get power
from their buttocks.
Even these city league players of softball
have enormous hams.
The lights coat each man
with a perfection you could live with.

If you spent all night in the park
the pleasure of the wind
would overcome exhaustion.
Or you could sleep
in the field of long grass
like a lost ball,
a home run.

When the game's over and lights are cut,
you think you see the shiny back of a coin.
It's only a cigarette package
catching a star
in its cellophane wrap.

for Jim Moore

Meditation on a Cold Rain

It seems as if an alarm
has been going off for days. Now silence.
The rain continues to fall steadily.
My seed packets say that most plants
in my garden need thoroughly warm soil.
I pull a wool sweater around me.
There is only one cookie left in the jar.
I say names out loud in the quiet room,
my own name, my mother's,
then the name of the man I love.
I hope the fish are biting for him up north.
I hope they will always bite and be fleshy and good.
I'm sustained by the quiet of a long weekend.
I am grateful to be speaking to myself.
I like the sudden cold of June.
I stay inside. I am inside. I am Margaret.
I am in love and alone.
I light candles. Steam folds onto the inside
of the windows. I can barely see the rain,
the wet slick streets, the mysterious yellow globe
of light in a neighbor's green room.
I think about movies of Japan.
I look out of myself for myself.
I do not like the thought of dying.
I am not afraid.
I carry solitude with me as a whole fruit.
I want an apple. I have an apple
corked by a tiny stem.

Owl of the Back Pastures

1.

With a wallop the magician opens
a folded top hat so large the night
and its torn pieces of stars fall in.
Our conversations rise and fall:
Do you call that star Venus?
My father says so. Do you still
climb rocks toward the stars?
Not since my friend died. Now I dance.

2.

Some moonlight caught in a cylinder:
that white finger of tree peeled clean.
The startled owl startles us.
Lifting from a stark tree,
its wings gulp air.
As if darkness swallowed
a bit of itself making the dusk
brighter, the bird's shape burns.
At the moment of takeoff,
the owl is all there is
with its gigantic wingspread and fright.

A glide of dun feathers, gone—
a bird of magnitude living its night life
in the solitary back pastures,
a vanishing act of great beauty.

In a Sheep's Eye, Darling

1988

Learning to Love by Hand

The adolescents, all blind,
cling to me as to a raft.
I walk them over to the sculptures,
lift their hands to greet the artist,
his figures, the ones the museum
lets us touch.

They begin with an elbow, a knee,
stroking as if it will release something.
When one discovers an arm,
she is so startled, she says *arm* out loud.

Hands begin to move faster
in a frenzy of touch.
Their fingers seek everywhere,
into the mouths of the men,
along thighs, in the little valleys
between the breasts of the women;
follow the belly down.

Watching makes me shiver
in the warm anteroom, a witness
to the lovemaking of those
who first learn longing from stone.

with gratitude to Cantor Arts Center staff

Looking at Lovemaking

Dreams did not make this moaning.
The couple in the next bunk did, two Dutch lovers,
she on her back with her knees drawn to her chest
like a doe stargazing,
and he, in a slippery, watery movement, tunneled
underground. Both swelling the room
with the wary, ragged edge of sobbing
without sorrow, like slowly tearing
old worn velvet.

This was in Greece in a cavernous co-ed hostel.
Through the shuttered windows,
the Plaka was still awake and the smell of lamb
sputtered oily and dark.
Up the hills, the Acropolis in its injured beauty
was locked for the night; the white limbs
that the sun polished held some of that light.

The love bandits made me edgy,
made me safe, their eyes like the dark of the moon
while mine shone in a pearled wonder
at these lying and locked bodies, as if
inside a bruised plum, the pit,
and inside the pit, the sprout of a seed
fingering its way through.

Giving a Massage

Here, the archipelago down your spine,
here, the dolphin dip of your lower back,
here, the firm reefs of your ribs,
here, the coral in your breasts,
here, the small shells on your fingertips,
here, the shoals near your temples,
here, the deep current of your mouth . . .

One Woman Telling: a Poem Sequence (excerpts)

1.

August

Summer is going, a lover slipped from the bed.
Last night I bought the weekend groceries near midnight.
The slim boy who carried them to the car
worked and hefted like a man,
said it was a fantastic night, softly warm,
said he didn't like fall,
said there's no mercy in winter.

Looking at his face, fresh as lettuce,
I wondered what was recalled in the lessening of the sun,
what he knew beyond the cosmetic tan of other boys
that made him mention mercy.

Around the long black lakes,
insects pant in the bushes,
little rough lungs.
A few cars cross paths
on the hot roadmap of the city.
Too late for movies, too late for bars.
People like me gone out for something:
cat food, milk and eggs, the paper,
contact with a stranger, this boy
who provokes a flamboyant tenderness.

In the garden, the last chrysanthemums
toss lavender pompoms into the air.

2.

December

We begin to barter. I'll give
you this poem, privacy, if
you'll give me a child.
You give me cleaning
and I'll give you a home.
You let me talk
then I'll let you alone.

We get angry, mouths like slashes
cut meals into little pieces.
The poinsettia's leaves are serrated knives.
We fight over a phrase in French.
Neither of us knows much French.
We stand in the kitchen, unable
to touch at all the right times.
I eat my words, bits of stale bread.
You tighten your hands and loosen them
like squeezing mud into the shape of sausage.

Packed full as boxes of Kleenex,
we take a hiatus from pain, hike
down towards the ice rink,
a cool metallic sheen under
a frosting of old snow.
Trees are stripped and gorgeous.
New snow tinkers with the air.
Hoarfrost thickens on every branch,
on the OK chain of the backstop
where a ballfield begins its buried sleep.

The yard next door is littered
with children making snow angels.

You pull me into the house
as if by the cross of bone above my heart.
Larger flakes buzz near the window—
a swarm of white moths.
And we hold each other
for an impossibly long last time,
our fingers blind as snow, falling everywhere
over our separate bodies.

3.

January

Some people establish their lives
like place settings sold only in pairs.
That easy.
Some do it with joy, their hands
on the spoons in the full drawers,
silver anchoring the room.
Married people have their reasons.

Your large hands grope, drop silverware,
crackling with despair.
You don't want to be fed on any schedule.
You don't want to feed.
You need to leave.
I need to let you leave.
Suddenly you're gone.

One spoon in my hand needs polish.
The tarnish smears off to reveal my face
upside down, of strange size,
the tiny pinhead and chin
pointed as a goatee.
Dipping my spoon's bowl into watery soup
I lay down my prayer:
that things are exactly as they must be.

I think of churches.
Of my life closing twice
as Emily said, dear Emily.
Is my god only a god of hard times?

I seek out churches,
pretend to be Catholic.
I want an ancient bloody Christ,
a burning heart and candles.
Each paraffined muscle in agony.
Loss is inside everything.
I fall to my knees, and further.

4.

February

Each night a new thing's in bed with me
and I wrestle for hours.
I want to fall away from bitterness
of defection.
I want to fall asleep.
There's no failsafe to the parachute
and I keep going down.

I rise in the morning with sorrow
I try to assuage
with bread, milk, coffee.
There is nothing to be done
but eat the sorrow with the bread.

I shake off my husk, wash my face,
turn on the radio, wait for the weather report
which is sure to be bad.
The house lumbers toward dawn
with me on its back.

The blast furnaces of the birds die down.
No fuel for them in the lumpish snow.
I find their stone carcasses.
I dress my ice in a suit,
collect myself into my car,
my soft hair bunned, my face made up,
my legs cool and useless in their shrill shoes.
A public self keeps on, keeps going.

So that I have something to do,
I save my grocery lists until Saturday.
I buy myself anthurium with their cold hearts.
I make long-distance phone calls,
let people hug me, tell me again
how much they like me.
I hang on to commitments, feed the birds,
refuse events I didn't like anyway.
I quit saying he was smart at games,
the best at Boggle.
I take down photos of him from the refrigerator,
stack them, face on face on face.
I put his socks in a garbage bag
and move into his bureau drawers.

The lantern of the moon shines.
I turn off all the lights in the house,
stay awake to watch the nothing,
the great whiteness, a whiteness to the bone.
Beyond whiteness, what?
The moon's skeleton, bone again.
What color's marrow?
A bone is Penelope beside the sea,
all her loyal muscles situated
in a posture of waiting.
In a chair, at some useful work
she wants to throw down, but holds on.
I want to be used, used well, made use of.
I want to be a useful quilt around a sleeping child.
Useful as a knife through beans' green sickles
for a meal of rich vegetables.
Useful as a man holding a woman,
giving her what she wants from him.

Under my clothes my small body
is a large surprise of bones and greediness.
Remember, I say to myself, you were often lonely
when he was here.
This loneliness is familiar.
I finger myself like prayer beads, without belief.

5.

May

A squirrel dallies on a limb, making it sway
as a child might, riding the branch to a gallop.
The backyard's leathery and patchy white.
I want to own all the corners of my house,
bake bread from honey and winter's wheat.
Goodbye to cold.
Welcome, spring, you wild blue kite.
Tomorrow the thermometer will break sixty.
The flowers catch the fever,
rush toward their season:
lilacs, shy guests, violets the size
of blue-tipped kitchen matches.
After its solid state, the earth
begins stretching for a new map.
The yard, a slick wet black.
The garden, where I dig, a wet and deeper black.
Under patched and dented snow,
green begins its old new song.
Tridents prick the dirt: daylilies.
Standing by the back window, I'm happy.
I think about it a while.
It's still true.

Seamstress

You give me your pants to repair.
You, who haven't been my lover for a long time.
I had nothing to do with the pants being torn,
for it was not from feeding you too much
or too little. Not for a project on my roof
you sacrificed the seam. It was not
in the haste of sexual play with me
nor in any way I saw or knew.

What have you been doing these days?
We have so much to talk about:
where these pants went
when I wasn't with them,
whom they met, where they were washed,
what hour of the night they were taken off
and where they were left when you went to bed.

Here is my hand. Here is the other.
I take your pants with your body absent from them
and I still repair the rents.
Here is my head bent over the tear,
and the fingers all together in one organization.
The frenzied end of the thread finally
licked into submission,
my eyes thread the needle first,
then the thumb and index follow suit.

I say nothing while I work. You, too, sit
with mouth pursed as if sewn that way.
My lips are chapped, feel like

the edges of cotton pulled by hand.
I'm torn up by happiness at being used.
This is a rip I don't know what to do with.

In a Sheep's Eye, Darling

All day in biology class he'd been looking hard
at everything put in front of him on the counter
as if he were starving for these sights:
a tree frog's beating heart, lichen from a tree,
even wax from his ear under a magnifying glass
made him bend lower, awed at the gunk
a body produces.

If this is what we slough off, how amazing
attached cells must be, he thought, and carefully
scraped some from the inside of his cheek.

The cells were blurred, like a smudged
charcoal drawing, just the way he imagined
cheek cells to be, not the precision of liver, not brain.
He knew he didn't know much about this,
and was probably wrong, but he loved
his own excitement, as if he were the first
person to open another in an operation
and discover all the organs under
a slipcover of fascia like tender offspring.

All this looking set him up to be stunned by the eye.
And he stared back at the big dismembered thing,
the way it sat in its socket like a pearl
in a soft oyster, like an oiled, see-through marble.
The cornea, tiny and perfect in its convexity,
and the lens, the way it flattened and thickened
in the center, white irregular filaments running
through it, as if some sight shattered inside
or some sight held, all sewn up.

The teacher thought it unlikely his wife
would share his thrill, but let him
carry the eye home in his backpack,
in the baggie left over from lunch, and the two
bent over it in the bright fluorescence of kitchen
and noticed the irrigation system of blood vessels,
and the soggy iris, and the cornea
and talked about what they could see being
only the tiniest part of the eye, and the eye
only a small part of the sheep, and the sheep
a small part of the farm and the Earth and the universe,
and they went to bed too awed to have sex.

That night he dreamed of the great grass
of sheep fields, the way it looked to the sheep
who stuck her head into it seeking
a particular blade, and the color green
welled up inside him like tears, and he awoke.

Going on Alone in the Great Conversation

Mother, you used to say that old
was just going on, no special feeling,
except of surprise.
You said that dead was a great conversation
continued. With the stars? I wondered.
With the living? With dreamers taken up
in sex or death?

Mother, the last time I saw you was last night
though you have been dead ten years.
Like fire in a paper, your face flamed,
each line and hair, both lips and hands
coveted in their sweet perfection.
Your only fault: you didn't stay
long enough. I want to talk with you.

With luck, your hands would pet my hair
which can never be touched enough.
With time, I could have smelled your smell,
yellow perfume, the dry flower of makeup.
Instead, after a glimpse of you,
I was like a child on the green grass
in the sputter of tulips, the parent departing
in the big black car.
I cry after it: *Come back.*
Take me with you. Me go along.

Me go on alone. Much later when
I am seventy, your age when you died,

old mother, I'll be your twin widow in the mirror.
We will both be wearing lavender,
absurd Easter hats and smiles because
we've faith in what's new and what is given.
Because we loved reading out loud,
the words, each one a new penny dropped in a jar.
Because we loved walking.
Because we have kneeled at each other's sickbeds,
and you passed on the little secret notes
and the gene codes, these bow legs from you,
these valentine eyes, this sentimental breathing.
Because we are each a word in a great conversation,
and the word is good.

Starting with the Vine

How I love the vine that grows beneath the north window,
a vine without much to say for itself,
just a few odd phrases of berries and leaves,
just that.
How I love the glitter on the cabbage, something like glass,
something like in a silver ring,
something like that.
How I love the way light hangs in the air of the room,
stillness falling in a particulate way,
the curtains, quiet and aired, the oncoming of fall.
How I love the photographs of friends,
my sisters with their glossy rose-red smiles,
the boys with their liver-soft baseball mitts,
the children of Roma who live in the South.
How I love how foreign my house feels
when the self subtracts its overbearing interests
except for love, love falling like light,
vacant and illuminating.

Milk and Tides

2008

In Response to the Door-Knocking Evangelist Who Asked: *What Saves You?*

Dusk doesn't, dawn does.
Morning splendor,
over and over and over again.
Newspapers don't, with their harpy
human interest stories.
But ah, coffee with milk in a plain white mug . . .

And graves in little cemeteries
in the country, on a hill, with a view.
It's good to think of spirits
having an eye for nature.

Sleep and dreams, the ones remembered,
even dreams about being chased because
that suspicion, that anxiety is given
its own body to run away.

Many books and almost every poem.

What saves often comes right
out of the blue, a sudden glimpse
from a bus in New York City
of a Lakota woman in a jingle dress.

Memory saves, especially random memory
that claims its own borders, its own orders,
makes its own metaphor.

A finger in an atlas seeking a town
on the west coast of Mexico

points to the face of a boy
selling candy on a bus a quarter-century ago
who couldn't talk, who moaned
when we gave him the wrong coin by accident.

Going to work and coming back saves me.
On Lake Street Bridge spanning the Mississippi,
four Catholic nuns—also actually sisters—
work for us all by waving placards:
Support our troops—bring them home.
I honk in solidarity.

Dinner at home last night:
exhausted with meetings and money-making,
I sank into a chair at a table
where all the food was prepared
by my husband and lit by candles:
salmon with basil and garlic,
deep green beans and a glass of wine.
Dave saying: *I'll rub your feet*
after dinner if you will just lie down
and put them in my lap.

The sight of my two sons saves me
even when they show me their backs.
Today that darkest month,
here in Saint Paul,
it's really cold, down
in the temperature teens.
My real-life teen heads off
to high school at 7 a.m. this morning,
coatless, gloveless, hatless,
his thick dreadlocks
powdered with snow.

Giving Blood

Could I be a Good Samaritan
who kneels beside an accident victim,
tears a tourniquet off my shirt to bind a leg?
To the telephone appeal, *Won't you save*
a life today by giving blood? I say *Yes.*

After I offer my name, secure a date
at the blood bank, my heart sinks—
shots, needles, and nurses produce
chills and a thready pulse.
Years ago I donated cup after cup
to my mother's thirsty leukemia,
AB positive, our types matched.
Back then, eyes closed, I breathed deeply
as the pulse inside my arm pounded
and the plastic bag filled with beet-red blood.

I don't want to do it, I whine to my husband
who doesn't tease or advise cancellation.
Why don't I go instead? he offers.
Returned from my appointment he kept,
I feed him tenderloin steak, I rub his back,
I cannot do enough for him.
He says: *Sweetheart, don't worry,*
I'll always bleed for you.

Basket, River

A baby placed
in a well-woven basket
of adoption
moves with the flow
that carries his little life
from one woman
to another whose arms
are ready to tend,
whose body has remained empty
of what she is in need of carrying,
who plucks a bundle
from among the bulrushes,
out of the water.

I stand at a river,
thinking of the woman
upstream, how in the middle
of hardship and loss,
she had faith
in a small basket, a kind river,
that someone with strong arms
would pull her son
from the current, lift him high,
raise him to manhood,
the beloved child of two mothers
who labored in different ways.

for women who have chosen
adoption for a child they bore

Marking Him

Does my little son miss the smell
of his first mother? I wonder
as the mewl of his mouth
opens toward a plastic bottle
that is not her breast.

Sudden new mother,
I bury my nose deep
into his skullcap of ringlets,
his starry cheesiness.

In her goodbye letter to him
sealed in his album
with a birth certificate, which now
lists my name as mother,

his first mother writes
she nursed him briefly
after he emerged into
the second room of his world

I think of milk, volcanic
and insistent, answering
the newborn's gigantic thirst,
a primal agreement between
generosity and greed.

Sometimes I press my nose
to the glass of that place
where a mother and my child

belong to each other;
I cannot imagine coming
between them.

But then I want to lick the baby
with a cow's thick tongue,
to taste him and mark him as mine
so if the other mother returns,
she will refuse her handled calf
smeared with my smell.

Deposed

With thousands of words at his disposal,
our three-year-old William, sovereign
of the house, loudly proclaims his opinions.
I don't like clothes with zippers or buttons,
he shouts one day as we help him dress.
I want a little family, just me and you two,
he insists as we try to warm him up
like cold milk to the idea of a sibling.

When William first peers into a green
blanket to find a new infant's face
like a fresh rosebud under leaves,
he glares, then marches off like a soldier
to damage something—a siege
that beheads a vase of flowers.

Although we show room on our laps
for two children, William begs:
Put that baby down or send him back.
Back where? we ask. *To his birth mother,*
he replies. *Tell her we tried him out*
and he didn't work.

From the kitchen monitor comes the sound
of baby Charlie cooing, then crying out sharply.
In the nursery, the unwilling older brother stands
crib-side, looking as if he'd like to banish
this tiny pretender to the throne.
His fingers are poised to pinch again.

Water Sign

Two-year-old Charlie loves water,

loves the force of water
in gutters, pipes, the second hose
bought to keep peace between brothers
who spray tomatoes with the intensity
of fire fighters at a five alarm fire,

loves the sources of water:
faucet, penis, rain, spit.

He longs like a pilgrim for wet places
where his worship is
complete submersion:
bathtub, swim pool, lake.

To praise water,
he secludes himself in the bathroom.
Ascending a stepping stool to the sink,
he opens valves to an endless rush
of new pressure in copper pipes.

So much water, why not share it?
Give it away until it seeps
through the floorboards,
showers into the kitchen,
fills the bowls on the table,
flows on the heads
of his amazed mother and brother
who do not immediately recognize

that grace might descend like this—
inconveniently—
from a complete enthusiast
who needs to be forgiven
for being generous
with whatever he loves.

First Day of Kindergarten

The bus steps are high, but William clambers up gamely.
Doors shut. He peers out a print-marked window.
From the street corner, I wave, wistful as a soldier's bride
as his bus pulls away and turns a corner.

At noon the yellow bus returns him
to the same place where I'm standing again.
He thinks I stood there all day, waiting in his absence.
When he finds out I left to play tennis,

his forehead crumples like paper in a wastebasket.
Now he knows I can move on my own without him.
Tears drawn from the well of desertion form in his eyes.
I'm his first love and his greatest disappointment.

Disguises

The smoke of roasted pumpkin drifts down the street
from jack-o'-lanterns burning in the night.
A little ghost trips on his sheet and cries out.

A pint-sized pirate, an alien who lost his flashlight,
and a famous baseball player run from house to house.
Watchful parents on foot trail the trick-or-treaters.

My son's friend wanted to paint his face black
to complete his costume as Jackie Robinson.
My son's real skin would have restricted him

to the *colored section* just two generations ago.
My own face appears in the mask of a fake mother
to my hopped-up-on candy boy.

Yet I wear the worried look of any real mother
aware of ragged unlit pavement, tampered loot,
and the terrible whiteness of my own skin as we pass
a scarecrow hanging by his neck in a front yard.

May 12, 2004: Twenty-Eighth Anniversary of My Mother's Death

My mother strokes my hair, pulls
a strand behind my ear. I wake
to heavy rain on the roof as if our house
were a toy washed under a waterfall.

At breakfast I tell my son that
I was with my mother when she died.
He asks how dying is,
and whether we die once,
the way we live once.
I could not answer, having just lost
my mother again in my dream.

I turn my wet face
to show my son—what?
If I were honest, I would say
I want him to see how deeply
he will miss me.

I would say sometimes
there is little we can do
for our children but go on living.
To be a tree in the rain for my son
to lean his whole nature against
until he knows how real he is
when I am gone.

Big Hair

In winter, ropey knots and dreadlocks
raise a lion's mane around his face.

He uses Bob Marley's photo
on myspace.com, not his own.

Now in hot spring, he scores his first job,
can't fit his 'do into the employee cap,

decides to have the wild bush
whacked, but declines the barber

whose shop attracts other young
black men with high style.

There's no escape for his father
who pulls out hair-trimming tools

inherited from his grandma.
William drapes a Batman cape,

sits on a kitchen stool so his dad can shear
the black mats that fall like Brillo pads.

The one now bald doesn't appear
to be the same boy: a soldier

could wear this chiseled head.
But look again, a soft-hearted youth

comes back thinking how to use
the surplus he raised and leaves behind.

Could it make a wig? he asks,
for someone like your mother

who got sick? I mask a smile,
imagine setting on her bare head

an ebony Rastafarian crown, bold
as shining gold bequeathed

from a grandson
she would have loved to hold.

Milk from Chickens

The day my son declared with hammerhead certainty
that milk comes from chickens was the day
I yanked him out of the city
and drove west to farm and prairie land.

Like a nail pried from hard wood, he complained
from the back seat, missing electronic games and TV.
Near the South Dakota border, he saluted
a McDonald's as we flew by.

I wanted my boy to take a turn lifting
barb wire to slip into open fields
keeping an eye out for the crazy bull.
I wanted him to hold a bottle for a lamb,

to feel the fierceness of animal hunger,
the suck of an animal mouth.
I wanted him to sleep in darkness encoded
with urgent messages of fireflies,

to see the bright planets in alignment overhead,
to stand on the graves of his grandparents,
dead so many years before he was born,
and to trace the names etched on granite pillows,

hard as the last sleep. How else to plant
in him the long root of plains grass,
help him reach water in drought
and know who his family is?

A Breeze Bends the Grasses

the kind my father picked
and brought to his lips to blow
the sound of a startled bird—

the cry his heart must have made
when he drove himself far
from us time and again.

Teach me, teach me
to make music
from plain grass.

Father showed me the way
to stretch a blade between thumbs,
to whistle a lone note.

He said: *That's it! Good*,
coaching me to climb a scale,
hit high notes,

practicing a melody
of happiness
he could not compose.

Why did I think all these years
only of how he was distant
then disappeared

and not of how he placed
his hands around mine
praying with me a green song?

Meadowlark Song

What hurt you today
was taken out of your heart
by the meadowlark
who slipped the silver needle
of her song
in and out of the grey day
and mended what was torn.

Life in Reverse

What if life were designed for us to arrive
when we're ancient, then grow younger?
If we start out as elders in our eighties
or nineties and change toward youth,
when our knees start working again
like well-oiled latches to a gate,
we do not protest grey hair or difficult digging
in the ragbag of memory for the right word.

When we become seventy years old, we're elated
that our bodies are as spry as they are
for we've passed down from real decrepitude.
We know what old age hath wrought—
disabilities, diapers, disease.
That's over now and we look forward
to decades of vitality.

We enter our sixties, that marvelous epoch
of activity, when we are now known
for something, when people see us as fluid,
not finished with our changes.
The driver's license we relinquished is back
in our hands. We take only occasional naps,
are into long walks, road trips and good works.
We have decent teeth and foods agree with us.

Our fifties—a really dreamy time.
Lovemaking is not an effort anymore.
Our flesh, though somewhat loose,
is more elastic than it used to be.

We cherish the work we do, whatever it is—
making things, going to meetings—
because we didn't get to do these things
back when we were eighty.
When stuck on the freeway,
we sing along to the radio.

When we grow back to forty,
we wear tighter, shorter clothes.
We can't get enough of color and travel.
As we build new rooms in our life,
we work on being generous because
we recall our old age when we appreciated
visitors at the nursing home, even if
they were the sons of the neighbors' son.

Thirty, we're ecstatically thirty,
even with our struggles.
Maybe the marriage isn't ideal,
and we have to move a few times, but
it's all experience, experience, and we thrive
on our power to learn.

In our twenties, we look down at our bodies
amazed how they shine with youth,
the flesh springy and firm
like a forest floor under pine trees.
We like sex outside, or on a table.
We welcome work and opportunities.

Next comes adolescence, which
used to be the best and worst of times,
because we felt so much

and knew so little.
But our past maturity gives
our teenage years ballast.
Now it's only the best of times.
We consistently make great decisions,
learn to play the flute,
show kindness to ourselves and our parents.
We are avid about education, use birth control,
enjoy in every way our glory.

When we get into grade school,
the great sex we used to have
when we were older is now
yucky to even think about.
Our parents tower over us.
Candy tastes delicious.
Nothing could be better
than playing kickball all afternoon.
We love our mother's voice
murmuring, her perfume,
the way stars are brighter
than they've ever been.
We can fall asleep anywhere
opening our hearts to dream,
and we wake up smaller,
believing in stories
where animals talk.

And then we are losing language,
but playing with all the toes on our feet.
Someone is usually holding us
and it feels so good to suck.
When we slide into the birth canal,

there's an agreeable sensation
of being drawn from a place
big and bright that often made us cry
into a cozy padded cave
where we rest with our ears
pressed to the pulse of a universe.
Then we are stilled with a lullaby
before lullabies had sound.

Earth's Appetite

2013

Truant

Our high school principal wagged his finger
over two manila folders
lying on his desk, labeled with our names—
my boyfriend and me—
called to his office for skipping school.

The day before, we ditched Latin and world history
to chase shadows of clouds on a motorcycle.
We roared down rolling asphalt roads
through the Missouri River bottoms
beyond town, our heads emptied
of review tests and future plans.

We stopped on a dirt lane to hear
a meadowlark's liquid song, smell
heartbreak blossom of wild plum.
Beyond leaning fence posts and barbwire,
a tractor drew straight lines across the field
unfurling its cape of blackbirds.

Now forty years after that geography lesson
in spring, I remember the principal's words.
How right he was in saying:
This will be part of
your permanent record.

Prairie World and Wanderer

Big bluestem and sedge, goldenrod and sunflower
gave us as children a place to go from light to dim,
from dun to emerald, exposed to hidden.
Above us, grasses displayed seeds to the sun.

When we were quiet, the small breeze and insects
made sounds as if saying *wish on this.*
A bird cried *come to me, come to me.*
The fields made a many-chambered house.

Pressing plants down, we carpeted floors.
In one room, we ate our sandwiches.
At the end of a tunneled corridor
we took naps, once finding where a deer

had tamped a sleeping space, still warm.
Once, we came across a stand of milkweed
with knots of sap in their umbels.
Ornaments hung from branches,

something folded inside, a drop that trembled
like a silent bell and broke, releasing
a butterfly with darning thread for feet.
The stained glass windows of its wings opened.

A monarch dried its wings of white, black,
and orange until it could flutter
like a tiny flag into the blue beyond
our mansion with its roof of air.

Bean Fields

They labor along the straight lines
of parallel rows, the farm boy, the town girl
earning an hourly wage for her college fund,
weeding, staying even with each other,
loving like crazy each other's smell.

He has the slight acrid burn of green leaves.
She, catmint—residue of shampoo—
her hair streaked shades of brown
like foxtail grasses in the sun.
His Tom body yowls in the backyard

of his brain that he wants that minty weed.
She longs for the end of the row
when they will sit in the bed of a dirty truck
against warm rubber tires and drink
lemonade with tongues so keen

you could map the exact spot where
the sugar of desire does its dream business,
where the lemon pulp—call it
her education plan, his religious training—
persists in its tart denial.

A bean in its ripe casing hangs on a stem,
three fuzzy lumps in its throat. One for the boy,
one for the girl, and one for how the hinge
of what might happen swings slightly,
opening here, closing there.

A Little Poem for Breakfast

The most radiant golden honey
came from my friend Lucinda
in a jar labeled "Dandelion Farm"
for that yellow star of the game
Do you like butter? Yes I do,
butter with honey on toast.
And I like how the jar holds
summer heat, the murmur
of bees, the dense scent
of a basswood flower
in the here-and-now
heaven of this day.

Norwegian Grandmother's Song

Little yellow canaries sing to me, sing to me.

Do you remember Stavanger
where the cold seas shook their sheets?

A rocking ship made me empty
my stomach into a pail over and again.

By water I came to this country,
by train I went to its prairie.

Oh, my husband, a beautiful Swede
who learned to lay bricks

for our living, was a tower
to my cottage. I clung to him

like a vine of pole beans to a stake.
Daughters we had, sons we had:

Ingrid and Kristin, Fredrik and Lars.
The Red River ran behind the house.

Giant cottonwood trees stood
at the banks like thirsty animals.

Little yellow canaries in your cage
sing to me in the warm kitchen.

Folding

I fold the futon bed where my son slept on winter break,
fold flannel sheets, touch fabric that touched him.

I press to my chest a stack of his T-shirts, warm from the dryer,
with his university's name festooned in maroon and gold.

A load of white laundry bleaches his undershirts, one sweat-stained
a sweet-corn yellow, the color of baby pee in cotton diapers.

I add two socks into a lump sum, press handkerchiefs into squares
the same size as notes slipped into his pockets by a smitten girl.

I gather, bend, and bag power cords that charge his gadgets.
Before I can enfold him in my arms and kiss him,

he packs his belongings and tall frame like a foldup ladder
into a friend's small car, waves and departs.

I wander through the house, visit his empty room,
find nothing left to fold except my hands.

How Does the Dog Spend Her Day?

I used to wonder when I was gone
eight hours at work, but now I know.
Since I lost my job, I find myself
following my dog's lead: wake late,
clean myself up, eat some crunchy food.
Then she and I go for a long walk
in the neighborhood, taking inventory
of the supply of squirrels,
noting wild rabbits so still
they advertise themselves
as lawn ornaments.

I, too, get my morning
and evening news from the air:
a nearby human smokes a pipe;
rain will arrive on wind
that fells the leaves.
The smell of another dog
on a telephone pole causes
my dog to tremble the way
a ringing phone startles me.
Sleep rules the house.
We both drool on our pillows.

I will get over this spell, I think,
I will answer ads, make calls.
But right now, I just whistle.
My dog comes at a trot
to look up at me, adoring
everything about me.
If only she were the head
of a company looking
for someone to hire.

What the Window Washers Did

They introduce themselves as Dave and Mike,
said no, they brought their own supplies
and equipment, said yes, pay in advance.
They circle the house, removing storms,
tugging at last year's ivy that cast its spell
of thatch across the east windows.

I open the door to Mike, watch
as he positions water bucket and rags.
Through grimed glass latticed with cobwebs,
Dave appears on the outdoors side.
As if starting a fight, both lift
their Windex bottles at the same time
and seem to squirt each other in the face.

The men, silent as mimes in a mirror,
their big hands tracing one another,
rub the surfaces of all the panes
until the glass squeaks and disappears.
Sunlight flies in on a bright carpet
and flings it on the floor.

And I Don't Know What to Say

June bugs bounce like pebbles
off the screens of open windows.
I turn the lights out and the night
asserts a larger presence.
Soon the moon will rise, full of itself.
You used to call at this hour,
Lone Star or Joe's Bar just closed.

You'd startle the phone
like a sleeping bird into sound.
No, I wasn't doing anything.
Reading maybe. TV.
Your voice was maniacally happy
or sobbing and moaning
like a witness to an accident.

You call daytimes now.
You lit three white candles
for sobriety today, say you feel
like a dry creek bed.
You want to be empty
and satisfied now the drink is gone.
You ask: *Will this be hard forever?*

At the Tea Garden

My friend and I mull over teas
displayed in square jars
with beveled glass labeled by type.
Each name seems part of a haiku:
"After the Snow Sprouting," "Moon Palace,"
"Mist Over the Gorges."
I'm drawn to green teas
with unoxidized leaves that don't wither,
hold their grassy fragrance
like willow under snow in winter.

The proprietor offers real China for the Chinese tea.
Animal bones, fine ground, give whiteness,
translucency and strength
to the porcelain that appears delicate,
resists chipping.
The rim of the cup is warm and thin.

My friend's lips are plush: her lovely
mouth opens to give advice I ask for.
We talk about memory of threshold events,
like a first kiss or a poem published.
She can't remember . . .

I tell her about my brother-in-law's
chemotherapy—his third bout of cancer.
He wants his family to put a pinch
of his ashes in things he liked:
his banjo, the top drawer of his desk, the garden.

I wouldn't mind becoming part
of a set of bone China that serves tea
in a cozy teahouse smelling of incense,
cinnamon, musk, and carved teak.
I'd like to be a cup brought to a small table,
to hear the quiet words of friends, to be held
in hands so close to lips
that breath on the surface of warm drink
makes mist rise over their faces.

for Sharon Chmielarz

Blood Oranges

A woman came on board the bus today
carrying blood oranges in a string bag,
her lips like red cuffs on the sleeve of her throat.

People in winter coats sit like spools of black and blue,
the shock of a Monday workday
freezing our morning faces.
I envy her, wrapped in a woven shawl
like a choir of crayons.
For months, I've tried to pull my heart up,
a stone from the well of disappointment.

Standing, she flirts with the driver in a language
that clicks like knitting needles.
Her voice filling the aisle could melt the blue slush
on the floor mats.
Laughter opens her mouth to a diva's O
plucking a high C.

Down the aisle she floats by our plastic pews.
As if happiness has a hand on her breast, as if
her body's infused with dazzled joy.
She is rickrack on a funeral dress,
a peacock's tail fanned against a gray wall,
a handful of bright corn to feed the birds.
She smiles with a candle's flame that doesn't fade
when it lights another.

The sun shoots golden arrows through
dirt-pocked windows.
I stop the bus with a tug on the cord.
The accordion doors open to a white carpet of snow.

Such Stuff as Stars Are Made On

The display of fireworks opens
umbrellas of flame and sound.
In a flash, our blanket is peopled,
then it's too dark to see faces—
only the dipper's white stars.

Flakes of soot and bits
of cardboard that housed gunpowder
fall on our heads.
It feels as though someone
is gently patting our hair.

This ash is carbon like our atoms
born in stars, recycled myriad times
over billions of years
until an expanding star
consumed them and exploded.

Instead of remaining in limbo
as interstellar dust, or traveling
to an unnamed planet,
we fell to a welcoming Earth
and gradually became ourselves.

Between Us

2016

Why Go to the Wilderness

When we walk, silence
walks with us.
Ropelike roots of trees
rig the rocky soil.
Might trip a woman.
Might roll a man with his backpack
like a beetle.

The vocabulary of wilderness
takes a long time to learn.

In the dark the sickle moon
looks left across the universe,
which means it will grow.
We sleep like pupas
in our down bags.

All night the river pours
its heart out over the rocks.

The Town of Annonay in the Rhône Valley

We'd driven all day on small roads
toward rain at dusk,
A little lost, tired, hungry, an argument
about to begin . . .
A small town showed up. With a hotel!

More good fortune: a bistro
across the central square
still serving near closing time.
Linen tablecloths, warm light.

When our French dinner came
the French chef came with it.
Assuming we were English
he asked, *Are you from London?*
My husband responded, *We're American.*

I'm so sorry, the chef said.
We laughed, yet a stab of fear—
he won't feed us as well.

Our main course came in a bucket—
what had we ordered?
With a ta-da flourish
the chef removed the top
to a cloudy opulence of mussels,
garlic cream and white wine,
shells split open to morsels
of going-to-heaven gray and pink.

We imagined we'd lived now and forever
in the village that vagabond night.

Old-Fashioned Names of Our Mothers

Our mothers died on the same day—
my friend's Hertha, my own Gladys.
When we cleared out their houses
we did not want to lose
any material—
not their stained aprons
worn to make solitary meals,
not bath towels or books
kept close like bedside nurses.

My friend had no home of her own.
Her mother's stuff came to stay
in my basement with my mother's stuff—
boxes labeled *Hertha's albums,*
Gladys's letters, Hertha's white gloves.

Some nights their objects call
our mothers back to try on hats,
whisper about husbands, children,
their lives of heartache and happiness.
When I reach out to them
they fade like photos
leaving everything in our hands.

for Yofe Johnson

Come Home, Our Sons

Not gunfire, but firecrackers
punctuate the dusk where I keep
lookout by the window for my son,
a young driver, to come home.

He was just a baby in the silver seat
of my grocery cart when a man
in uniform muttered:
I can't get over a white woman
with a black kid.
I've never gotten over the beauty
of my son, his plum-dark eyes,
never gotten over fear for him.

This poem is for my son
off to the movies in his first car,
Three times in the past month
police pulled him over.
Ashamed, having raised him
to be proud, I now plead for
subservience, his voice low, hands
visible, movements meek and slow.
I can't share my own talisman
for safe travel, only a week
checklist for how to survive.

This poem's heart goes out
to other mothers who cannot sleep,
who keep me company
listening into the night.

Where is a force to watch over sons
like ours, a power that escorts
them back unharmed?
We are waiting for car lights to beam
in front of our homes, for the cars
to belong to our sons, and our sons
to still belong to this world.
We are waiting.

dedicated to Valerie Castile, Philando
Castile's mother who said, "African
Americans are being hunted every day."

Knitting Pattern

She took me in hand, taught me
to knit wool from lambs
she raised to sheep.

With my torn jeans and dirty face
I was wild as a barn cat.
She gave me the quiet
of her farmhouse, helped me cast on
into the realm of soft clicking,
elbows moving up and down
like bellows breathing.

I learned the delicate dip and dive
of needles and the patient way
to stockinet, garter, seed.
How not to drop a stitch.

Now a neighbor child
whose mother says can't sit still
comes to me for lessons.
Her feet don't reach the floor
but the scarf grows long
on her needles.

After we finish a session
we go out on the back porch
to bark and yowl, as I did
with my teacher who said:
Calm down a bit
but don't get prissy.

That Summer Abroad, Joanne

Have we ever been so free as then?
We'd change destinations
on a whim, Rome one day,
hitchhiking to Brindisi the next.
The cheap berth on a ferry to Greece
meant sleeping on the deck by Italian boys.
Remember their garlicy breath?

I want to call you up right now,
buy one-way tickets to Athens
where we'll board the boat
to the island of Skyros.

We can take turns going to the bakery
for warm bread at dawn,
wearing cotton shifts
we slept in like virgins.
The sun runs its hands up the hillside
to each white house.

Belongings

After being a student, then an hourly worker,
I became a career girl and earned real money.
I could leave behind a provisional furnished apartment
with its stained curtains, butt-burned table
and Goodwill mattress I was never sure about.

I'd been dealt a good hand of dollars.
I bought a house with an attic, a basement,
and a skirt of flowers.
Freely I spent on white paint, silver knobs
on kitchen cabinets, and a corduroy sofa
that pressed wrinkles on my face when I napped.
A bureau displayed photos and framed mottos:
If only one prayer, thank you will suffice.

Do I regret the down payment, fixtures, fittings,
furniture, years of mortgage?
Would I take anything back?
No, I would not. I meant it all,
every purchase.
I still welcome the weight of things
that encumber and root me on this Earth.

What the Hostess Doesn't Say on Holidays

Farewell, family. I'm exhausted,
at the end of my rope,
of my line.

I've been up since five o'clock
making Grandma's dill bread
and Aunt Alice's apple crisp
with my amazing stove.

My hand-me-down table
is set with good wares.
You occupy all my rooms.
The noise of shared histories—
all the voices—
makes me frantic.
I choose to chill
in the mudroom
with empty wine bottles.

Please! Stop gathering,
say goodbye
to those stories,
jokes, the counting
of grievances:
You always were the one . . .
Don't you remember?

The cold feels good out here
and fierce.
My heart is a pure diamond
on which no family
will scratch its mark.

Day After Daylight Savings

Blue numbers on my bedside clock
tell I forgot to change the hour.
This sets routines on haywire.

Like a domestic goat staked
to its circle of browsing.
I don't do well untethered.

I have no hunger for early dinner,
become confused by the sound
of children who seem out

too late for a school night.
They've found an extra helping
of daylight to romp on new grass

and can't contain themselves,
strip off jackets, scatter
like a rag of ponies.

Whatever time says,
their joy insists
on springing forward.

Happy Day, with Egg

An urban chicken named Nancy
nesting in the birdbath
laid an egg today
then walked around the yard
with a fluffed chest
holding high the crown
of her red comb
loudly clucking about herself
and her marvelous achievement.
Exactly how I feel
when I write a new poem.
Tonight at supper I'll celebrate
with a little omelet.

Lapses

Sometimes a word is obedient
and comes: *good word, good dog.*
Sometimes the word cowers in a corner.
A friend might fill in the blank for me.
Or I mime action that brings laughter.
Circling my hands around
my waist conjures up *belt.*

Or I invent a description.
When I can't recall *air bags,*
I say: *The car's exploding pillows.*
I say: *You know those little white barbells?*
To which my husband says:
Do you mean Q-tips? Yes!
I'm looking for Q-tips
and friends' names and books I read
just last month or last night.

It's easy to remember
the name of the blonde boy
who moved away in third grade
and the title of the first movie
that made me cry.
Like an old horse to its salt lick,
my mind ambles to essential nouns:
rain, apple, sleep.

Let Me Return as a Tree

The one outside our window—your favorite,
the sugar maple that hosts a congregation
of birds in spring, drapes its leaves
across the streetlight in summer.
You would study me for changes as you did
in life: is my color more yellow, more green?
You would see me blaze in fall flame,
diminish to twigs, as I may have done in dying.

I will watch your sweet owlish face
for signs that you are finding pleasure
in a solitary life. Do you feed yourself well,
enjoy company—our friends, our sons?

In spring each of my origami leaves unfolds.
A runnel of rain pours down my trunk.
I see your eyes enlarged by glasses
looking at me with kindness. I didn't know
until I wrote this poem how much I love you
and it's not too late, not too late to tell.

Shelter

2020

Art

As the sun begins to build its house of gold
an artist is called to her window.
Alone in the attic of creation
free to leave her body, lift bird-like
and settle on bare branches,
she can portray what is before,
within or beyond herself.

With pencil, paper, color,
she paints an upside-down bowl
of blue essence some call heaven.

Anne Frank, too, in the bolt-hole
of a tiny annex found her patch
of sky and shared her vision.
She wrote in her diary: *Think
of all the beauty in yourself and
everything around you and be happy.*

for Sharon DeMark

Belly

Hey little astronaut
floating in the fluid
of inner space
attached to the mothership
by a cord, cosseted
and coveted, you
human-to-be
within your protected
red universe
of heat
and heartbeat
come, we're eager to see
your face when you complete
your marvelous
mission
and are equipped
to live here on Earth.

Canopy

Like a child I sit down, lie back,
look up at the crowns of maple,
needled spruce, and a big-hearted boxwood.

Fugitive birds dart in and out.
In the least little wind, birch leaves turn
and flash silver like a school of minnows.

Clouds range in the broad sky
above Earth's great geniuses
of shelter and shade.

for Norton Stillman

Porch

Even this hot summer, it happens
the porch has its Saturday mornings
of ease, its trees and bird song through the leaves.
We drag chairs to the open air,
settle in to watch walkers parade by
on city sidewalks with ears pressed
to the seashells of their small phones.
Sometimes we call out to a friend or wave
to the red-haired toddler in a stroller waving at us.

Even in this heat, everyone else seems intent
on important business ahead.
The dogs pull on their leashes and girls jog past
leaving a trail of glittering laughter.

We're at the age we don't mind
being passed by; ambition has left us calm
and easy in our wicker chairs, books in our laps.
We just want to linger on the porch
as if on vacation, observing people
and scenery part of and apart from us.
The porch with its deck and white balustrades
carries us like a boat on smooth water
toward the long afternoon.

Sanctuary Church

We came here in the rain. I brought my doll.
The room is little and clean. Sometimes
there is singing of many people in the walls.
Shh, Mama touches fingers to my lips. It's a secret
how we got to this place.

We used to live by Grandmother. My school
had a red door. We slept on the floor
when guns shot. The coo of pigeons came in the light.

We hide because we have no papers.
The women with food bring papers for me
to draw on and crayons bright as gold.
My mother says that the women
have hearts of gold I cannot see.

Someday we will leave for a house with no fear.
It will be good like eating when you are hungry.
And this is how we live. And this is how we live.

after Randall Jarrell

Summoned

2021

Born into One Body

Isn't it odd how we're born
in one country
and not another,
could have been any other
color instead of what
we are? We might speak
Parsi and send our dead
to the place of birds.
Strange that we work
at desks in cool rooms
not making clothes
in factories, sweltering,
being slapped or called
donkey or *dog*.

What if we suddenly changed
into another, disappeared
into a labyrinthine souk,
wearing shorts and
a baseball cap, emerging as
a man in a djellaba
or a woman with red
embroidery of henna
on her hands?

We'd sit in the shade
of a palm tree, feed dates
to a child never seen before
but surely she is ours.

Another Day of Being White [In South Dakota]

My husband ambles into the kitchen
to help with the stew—
its plenty of meat and fresh beans.
I say I have *Indians* on my hands
when I meant *onions.* My eyes water
with the odor of white rings
around my fingers or maybe
I'm crying because the two dollars
I gave to the worn-down man
with his cardboard sign was almost nothing.

Feelings churn and I mistake words
as if on laughing gas given
to a woman with a broken tooth
who could afford pain-free repair.
My friend Roy said gaps and stubs
of teeth tattletale of growing up poor.
He smiled with his mouth closed.

My tongue slipped onto *Indians*
because deep into the night
I'd read a book about Wounded Knee
then attended a workshop
about the trauma of being white,
how we carry in our bodies
collective *quilt*, I mean *guilt*.

I twirl a confirmation ring
on my finger, its rose gold

grape leaves from a mine
in the Black Hills where
prospectors trampled treaties
making it possible 70 years later
for my family to build
a house on South Dakota soil
in a land grab we didn't want
to ponder. Sometimes my mother
sent money to Pine Ridge Reservation
along with secondhand clothes.

Another Day of Being White [Dog Incident Report]

My goldendoodle puppy, apricot-colored,
looks like a dust mop on legs.
Rosie adores everyone, wants to lick hands,
is friendly indiscriminately with all humans
in her orbit, lucky little star, recipient
of sunny attention from many strangers
until today when I errored (as the training book
calls it), let out the leash five feet
and unheeded her dash through the doorway
of a bus shelter where a man sat
slumped smoking a cigarette.

When she came at him, he leaped to his feet,
onto the bench the way fire jumps,
his dark eyes on her, his face a rictus of terror.
Was he yanked back to facing a mouthful
of guard dogs' teeth? Or to a traffic stop
with K-9 cops who call Black men *dog biscuits*?
Maybe he's been warned of feral dogs and rabies.
Need I tell you I'm a white woman
in a mostly white neighborhood,
and like the puppy, I'm used to being liked.
He is a Black man uninterested in the apology
I try to make from a distance. Was our
encounter about race? Could he just
be a guy with a primal fear of dogs?

Saint Francis Pet Cemetery

Under our dog's tongue
the stone of a tumor.
We always fed her dry food
but now offer a death row diet,
whatever the pooch wants:
meat scraps from our plates,
casserole with rice.

We walk slowly, let her go
unleashed, stopping in a pet cemetery.
A granite statue of Saint Francis
stands watch over the tombstones.
He who tamed the wolf
believed in the souls of animals.
He raises his hand to bless them all.

We'll be back soon to plant ashes
among the grave markers remembering
Teensy, a terrier, Busy Bob, a hamster,
and on a cross made of Popsicle sticks:
Spaz the guppy, swimming forever.

Summoned

One early morning with a few strangers—
white, Black, brown—I walk
in silence to the crossroads
where George Floyd died.
It's filled with balloons,
flowers woven into blankets,
stuffed bears, and among many,
this handmade sign:
All mothers were summoned
when George Floyd called out for his.
My thoughts are with my son,
who sizzles with fierce words,
not just for the policeman
who arrested him after curfew,
handcuffing him with zip ties.

He's also angry at me because
I adopted him or maybe because
I'm white like the cop and he is brown.
He refuses therapy, is moving out
in the middle of the pandemic
with no plans of where to live.
At home, in another shadowy dawn,
a family of crows argues.
Soon it will be light enough to see
how the maple hangs her head
over the grass.
I can't imagine the future for my son,
so I look backward to see
a small boy's beautiful body

walking into a swimming pool on tiptoe.
As the water gets deeper, he points
his nose up like a fox smelling the air.
He has always been audacious and brave—
it's something to hold onto.

Behold December

To be held, the minister says, *we must behold.* Tonight
I behold a fringe of frost on the windows where
candlelight stutters. Although weary, I drive through
the dim evening to visit a friend who has fallen on ice.
I behold the winter's dark coming and the fear of being
brittle-boned and alone.

On my friend's kitchen counter squat numerous glass
bottles and jars—containers, she tells me, from cleaning
her fridge, items past their expiration dates. *I hope we last*
past our shelf lives I joke, and we laugh. With no garbage
disposal and no dishwasher, my friend lacks equipment
to make it easy to scrub contents and ready the glass to recycle.

Perhaps it was the kindness called for at church or what
I know as my attachment to order that prompts me
to swoop up a bag of her half-filled bottles and jars to clean
at my own house. At home I'm surprised to behold
my adult son around whom a confusing and smokey cloud
of alcohol and anger drifts. I stiffen in his presence.

But lo, he's eager to help, lifts the bag from my arms
like a baby. He twists tops off jars that my arthritic hands
can't manage. He shakes red globs of ketchup into the sink.
We hover over the cauldron of a garbage disposal whirling
yellow chutney and fish sauce, rancid salad oil and green
peaches. We pinch our noses against the smell, laugh,
look outside where the lightest snow has begun to fall.

From a reflection in the window I behold:

Side by side
our shoulders touching,
two animals yoked together.

Grief

Green tea in the night before first light.
It's early, even for me.
How to hold the day
in my arms like a day-old baby
struggling to survive,
her curled fingers tiny as wren's feet.
I dreamed my dog
smelled cancer in my throat.
I dreamed my son
was back in his room,
playing solitaire
and not in a jail cell alone,
his phone card spent.
I know how one hand holds the other
orbiting each knuckle with a thumb.
I'll do what I need to do.
I'll fall softly as light rain on myself.

Paint for the Baby's Room

Tumbleweed, Ostrich Egg,
Algonquin—who dreams up
these names for paint on color strips,
labels, and formulas for mixing?

Who thinks of Homeland,
Cedar Chest, Alameda Red?
Of Raleigh Green, good for exteriors,
and Lemongrass for trim?

Poets! To name their products
paint companies must hire those
who know the color of words
and how to be brief and stunning.

Water Mirror is light gray
like a May rain or pencil tips.
The beige of Oatmeal Bath can accept
cotton curtains' upbeat blue.

In a room of Yellow Water Lily,
a little boy lies in a crib.
He is the hue of Warm Earthenware
with a mouth of Deep Mulberry.

Another Day of Being White [With a Neighbor Who Forgets I'm a Black Kid's Mother]

A neighbor leans conspiratorially
out his car window to tell me
as I weed the boulevard:
There's a prowler around—
Black kid seen casing the alley,
taking pictures. Just warning you.

Acid in my throat almost burns
through superficial social skills
girls like me learned from mild
mothers who swallowed anger.
I say: *You're talking about my son.*

We had believed he was safe
this summer with his job
for the community council
that sends him with a camera
to take pictures of gardens
worthy of awards.

Another Day of Being White [At the Nail Salon]

Black-haired workers in nurse-
white uniforms (USA size 0)
perch on low stools.
They speak their own staccato
behind paper masks,
ask *too hot?*, say *twenty dollars.*
Moving lips make a slight tremor
when they laugh.
Larger women (I am one)
on overstuffed vibrating
chairs present bunioned feet,
toenails like bits of seashell.
Lang Vu employs a pumice
stone, warm towel for drying.
I pick pretty pretty paint
(Strawberry Summer Burst),
sigh with satisfaction.
Workers here grasp
thc long tail of an old war.
We get this kind tending.
They get this kind of work.
I tip well out of gratitude?
generosity? guilt? I place
money in the cupped hands
of a young woman
and leave on good feet
in good sandals.
No bombs fall from my sky.
My water's not tainted

by Agent Orange.
My children play in fields
free from unexploded ordnance.

Red Dress

In the back of the attic closet
on a rack of old duds for Goodwill,
a dress still hangs, brief and bright,
pert, a ruby coronation.

A man at a swing dance whispered:
You shine in your orbit
as you twirled and the skirt
fanned out to your thighs.
Later you leaned back on a hot car's hood
to drink a long and starry kiss.

In a mirror when you hold the dress
against your figure, its svelte shape
won't stretch to cover you,
wide where you used to be slim.
Parts of you that lifted and were light
are now among fallen things.

You could just keep a swatch
of fabric to pin in a picture frame
with a bit of slippery wedding gown
and a snippet of baby blue flannel.
But you want the memory whole
of being wrapped in the silk
of a red hot damn of a dress.

Stroke

It was a mild one, they say I'm lucky,
my husband tells me over the phone.

It was only yesterday he saw
everything doubled—
a book, his finger, my face.
Was the trouble his tired eyes?
A call-line nurse urged emergency.

I drove him to the hospital's red door,
no farther. COVID: no visitors.

All night alone in our bed
built for two, I tried to hush
the insistent insomniac of worry.
Would my husband walk again,
talk, know who I am?

An MRI image of his beautiful brain
showed a small region gone dark forever.
What memories might be lost?
Jokes that made his students laugh?
The first meal we ate together?
Our son's favorite tune on his trumpet?

This morning my husband aced
cognitive tests, counting down
from one hundred by sevens,
making a long list of words
that begin with the letter m:

morning
music
mountain
mystery
moon
more . . .

Aubade in January, with Cardinals

Shovel the driveway, salt the ice.
I roll like a wave to your side
of the bed, against your back
with its archipelago of bones.

Friends send pictures of themselves
standing by tumbleweeds in Texas,
lolling on a beach blanket in Florida,
wide smiles lit from within
like jack-o'-lanterns.

We mate for life and do not migrate,
live by the great clock
that appears earlier each day.
Weather will change its cold ways:
hepatica's purple bloom up
through patches of melting snow.

This morning we watch a male cardinal
with his punk hairdo crest
place a black sunflower seed
in his mate's mouth the way
we might feed each other dark chocolate.
Sweet-sweet-sweet calls the cardinal.

Audubon's *The Birds of America*, Color-Plate 211

If you, too, dream to be born again
as a bird, wouldn't you want to be
a great blue heron, rare vagrant
wintering in the Azores and coastal Spain,
snacking on shrimp while wading
on long, beautiful legs? And if

you loved your life as a human who
sheltered in a small house by a lake, you
could summer there again, nesting
in the white pine, fishing on the shore
in the blue Zen of stillness when early
morning ambers the eastern sky.

The Call of Glacier Park

2022

Air of Gods

When the park was young
and you were young and wild, too, Mother,
you came wearing a velveteen jacket
and slight shoes as if in a fairy tale,
as if for a dance. When glaciers
were still many and large. When
you came to the park by train.
Insubstantial air made you and your friend
pant as you hiked. You ate
huckleberries picked in alpine meadows,
your mouths dark with juice.
You drank water from one
of a hundred silver streams.
On the Lincoln Pass near Gunsight
a storm gusted around the cliffs
releasing its cargo of hailstones and rain,
cold and fog. You'd gone up
into the mountains. You got your wish
to walk in clouds.

Now the mountains you climbed
call us toward turquoise lakes
and heights where we, too, breathe
aether, the air of gods.

The meaning of the word "aether" has been in flux for almost 3,000 years. In ancient times, Greeks used it to describe pure air breathed by gods in upper realms.

Blue Tent

We heeded the call of mountains
arrowed with evergreens
pointing up, up.

My backpack carried its share
of our camping equipment:
lantern, propane stove, nylon tent.

We studied each campsite
for a stoneless bed and a tree
to hang the food pack.

Tent poles, stakes, ropes fit
into pockets and grommets and ground.
Lifting the tie beam

made the tent happen all at once
as if we pulled a home
out of a hat.

Inside the open flap, packed goose down
of our sleeping bags began to loft,
two zipped together as one.

Before sleep, for a final pee,
I stumbled a polite distance out
into the thickening dark

but not too far
to lose sight of lantern light
in the luminous blue tent.

Hiking Gear

> *"Part of the path is quite rocky and with my miserable shoes it wasn't so good. I fell once and cut my hand and got pretty dirty, but I already was dirty so a little more didn't matter."*
> *–from Gladys Johnson Hasse's diary, 1926*

My mother didn't have equipment
we have now to travel miles
into rough terrain with maybe bear
and bad weather around each bend.

Without our insulated footgear
and shock-absorbing midsoles,
her feet grew cold, her teeth chattered.
She slipped and tripped on the steep
way down to Lake McDonald.

She did not have, as we do,
warm lightweight jackets
protecting us from chill and rain
with pit zips and a hood
for weather's change of mind
from sun to rain to snow to cloudy cold.
She could not see more
than eight feet ahead
on a skinny trail 6,000 feet up,
one stumble meant a fall
and a scream into fog below.

For her, no Camelback pack
with baggies fat with GORP,
fruit, crackers, cheese,

water in hydration packs
and a spout inches from the mouth.

For her, a thin jacket,
a meal of one Hershey bar shared
with her friend,
half a wet sandwich,
wild berries picked
from their bushy abundance.

For her, water
from ice cold streams
where she went down
on all fours to drink.

Gunsight Pass: Elevation 6,946 Feet

As we climb we absorb light, like flowers.
Far below by the cold shoulder
of a small lake, two slight tents are pitched.

The wind updrafts valley air scented
with white pine. A hawk pierces the quiet
with its scream. Two mountain goats bleat.

We wish we had goats' nimble way
of stepping up the steep, narrow paths,
steady on their four cloven hooves.

The goats continue climbing unmarked trails.
Turning back to look at us, their faces,
bearded and bony, seem like those of wise men
we'd like to follow to where Earth ends in sky.

Wilderness of Last Resort

We don't know how to live with dying glaciers.
Maybe we don't belong here either, grouchy
with heavy backpacks and hungers.
Harsh words unfurl like smoke.

We walk the long line of a trail trying
to look at things up-close where miracles are.
An ostrich fern bears fruit shaped like the whorl of an ear.
Instinct tunes a long-married couple to turn together
toward the purl of water over rough stone.

When we sigh into silence, the forest disturbed
by our human huff and gabble stirs.
Wands of branches sway and the movement of small creatures
catches in the corners of our eyes.

White moths hatching from invisible places begin
to crawl over fallen logs, up tree trunks, the legs of our pants.
Chiffon wings open, close, dry.
Hundreds cluster on our shirts like boutonnieres
of wild flowers or ghostly fans ready to fly toward light.

We don't know much but the Earth knows everything.

Moose

Other tourists' silence stilled our voices.
They were studying something in the marshy waters
we couldn't yet see.
A child's cry quieted in its throat,
a stone dropped in water.

An animal rose from its knees in the lake,
water pouring from its shoulders, its back.
A massive bull moose stepped out
of lake onto shore,
mud on its back, bracelets of milfoil
on its ankles.

Against a backdrop of watchful ancient pines,
he crossed the trail in front of us
holding his long and homely head high,
his ivory antlers like a tray of melted candles.

He was unexpected, something I needed
that afternoon in my mother's mountains,
when thirsty, hot, and seeing
in my sister a resemblance to her,
then missing my mother more.

Grief, does it never end?
Alongside memory, love and beauty
grief breaks us into our fullest being.

Now My Mother Is

Now my mother is the mist of clouds
in the high peaks
and the yellow rose in a garden,
the gingham apron
left behind in a closet.

Now she no longer has her hands on the T
handle of the red wagon nor the O
on a Scrabble board.
We play her favorite game, pull for her to win.

She is not baking brown bread
in the kitchen, not sitting up reading in the red chair
until we come home.

She is where we go when in need
of water from streams we belly down to,
of singing as we walk recalling words
of animal songs—the fox on the trail,
the goat that flagged the train.

We find her here in cool mornings,
our breath sharp as pine needles, at night,
around the stove blackened with the work
of its making heat and meals for a hundred years.
If she were a sound, it would be part wind in the pines,
part love song, pet names, and poetry.

Belongings

2024

Householding in the Time of COVID

Our unfenced fields of days without plans
or people outside ourselves remind us
of Keats' *silence and slow time.*

Things broken stay broken.

Sequestered time unspools.

We sit for hours watching small dreams
and dramas unfold—the cat batting
dust motes in sunlight, the flit
near the window of gorgeous birds
we've only lately learned to name.

We make a library of our house
reading what and however long we like.

Stretched out on a rag rug made
by my mother in the century that made us,
we study family albums closeted for years.

The forgiving animals of our bodies
kept busy with calendar, kids and work
now know what to do without.
We sleep more, eat less,
walk for solitary hours
and look at the world
in light of a first dawn.

Waking Up Without

Alone and curled
on my side of the bed
I watch dark change
to milk, then grow golden.
It's early morning
and visiting hours
do not begin
until ten o'clock.

I unbraid strands
of birdsong
the open window brings—
a cardinal's cry,
the robins' all bright
a-twitter in bushes
that hug the house.
Will anything other
than my clothes
hug me today?

In a hospital
windows stay sealed.
It's been five days.
You must get better.
You must return
to share our bed,
hear birds stir
in the morning,
say my breath
reminds you
of damp leaves.

Worry Beads

I worry about David Copperfield
as a ragged boy on his walk to Dover,
his few guineas stolen before
he left London. I agonize over
my son, living his 45 days of jailtime
in our basement, an electronic monitor
on his ankle, a breathalyzer
by his pillow. Will little David find
his aunt? Can my son keep a cork
in the bottle? Today the weather
troubles me, too. Heat and turbulence
signal things to come. What does
the relentless wind mean to do
to the red pine struck by lightning,
its top leaning toward the north star?
Ice melts at the poles, seas rise.

By complaining does it change
the weather? my sister used to ask.
I'm concerned I'll forget
this phrase, along with the date
and place I was born.
I brood over how to pronounce
draught and *Worcestershire.*
Apathetic or cruel people refused
to help David Copperfield
and my friend when she wandered
from the senior center.

I worry that the divide in our country
gaps too great to be stitched together

like a giant scar, that alcohol
grips too tight for my son to escape.
Many craven or credulous citizens
with guns live in our country.
Where is a north star to chart
our journey toward a better place?
I wring my hands, I write.

Coming Clean in a Finnish Sauna

Inside a box of toasty cedar
you drip like a salty sea
onto blistering benches.
Your arms, your belly
greasy with sweat.

The temperature grills—
how high can you go,
how long can you stay?
You stand it, you sit in it,
you lie on towels
while heat soaks
organs and bones.
Your hair's so hot
it could flame you
into a redhead.
Eucalyptus air
sears your throat.

When you must burst
out the door to put
out the fire, you fling
your body into a bank
of bitter snow.
Your skin almost sizzles.
You feel fierce
as the eye of Arcturus,
a giant red star
in the night sky.

Good Enough

Do we worry too much
about the weather, about our children?
Worry changes nothing,
just nicks the hours near midnight
as we nightmare reasons
our son hasn't come home:
spinout on ice, overdose.

When he arrives after curfew,
bleary-eyed but whole,
we hug him instead of scold.
Choose your battles
parenting books advise
as if we're working at war.

Once we slept through a tornado
that ripped up the neighborhood,
waking in a house that endured the blast.
We said *a miss is as good as a mile.*

Let's not *sweat the small stuff*—
dented fender, spoons we gave away
before we knew they were silver.
Our lives are almost as good
as we want, in other words,
good enough.

A Garden of Her Own

She is always in bloom,
whatever task she takes on,
whatever age she becomes.
I call her Flower Girl
because I think of her in a garden
of her own making—like the garden
where youth turns wise and healthy,
or a kitchen garden
where the best food seems to sprout
like magic beans into deliciousness.
She goes down on her knees
in the rich loam of living.
Friends, family, work,
travel, photos, books, birds, dogs—
she honors all.
We know her steadiness, and her delights.
How appealing she is in her greening growth.
What she touches becomes fruitful,
more tasty, more beautiful—
it becomes whatever it meant to be.

for Patsy Noble

Neighborly Advice

By nine in the morning
my neighbor has pulled up
her bedroom shade
on my side of her house.
By this, she signals she's still alive.

At ninety-five, you never know,
she told me in early summer
when we made a pact
across our backyard fence,
her house dress an easy-wash
polyester, her face round
as a warm peach.

At seventy, I must seem
full of ambition, practically
a youngster in her eyes.
My garden's a roll call
of orderly vegetables in long rows.
In the fall I plan to put up
jars of pickles, squirrel away
bags of dusty potatoes.

My neighbor's done planning.
Her yard, all flowers,
delivers a disheveled riot of color.
Not sure she'll see October,
she says *it's best*
to just take what comes.

Things Are Always Falling

Nowadays, things are always falling.
Oak leaves fell into the lake today,
golden rust making a ring around
the shore. Crabapples wizen,
stop holding tight, carpet
the yard in random mushy patterns.
Our hearts sink, we say, when bad news
strikes. Tears fall. Another season
of losses: a chemo-ed woman, her hair,
a man going deaf, the nightjar's call.

As we age, life keeps carrying out
its calculations and subtractions.
We're told to rid our house of rugs
that trip us up, cause us to fall down.
Our skin thins, breasts slacken.
We wane like the moon. Falling stars
scratch the night sky. Our memories
fade and fail. And one by one
we say goodbye to people we loved.
One by one by one.

Kinship of Animals

I must forgive myself for believing my friend a bit
dotty to love her ragged tabby so much she stayed
home from vacation in Europe to drip medicine
into its yowly mouth. And for making fun of a D.A.R.
dowager who wanted to will money to a beloved
parakeet named Peter. I pitied a man his obsession
for horses whose names he had tattooed up
and down his arms. All this love, money,
attention expended on animals instead of people,
I thought wrong.

My judgments softened when a dog came along
with snap-black eyes, a happy grin, sweet breath
and disposition. Who can explain exactly why
we love what we love? Now I, too, am a human
devoted to the life of a creature from another realm.
Here comes pooch Rosie now, watching me
for clues of how we can be good to each other.
We have simple needs: food and fresh water,
play in the backyard. We walk in the woods,
sleep in one another's animal presence.

By Hand

My dog loves ACE Hardware for treats
the high school boy who mans the check-out counter
provides provided she sits, she lies, she shakes.

After I pay, home go a cache
of silver-colored objects to keep
the house in shape: valves, sheers, screws, pipes
and an implement with a most impressive name:
three-axis
  metal
    spirit level
      bubble vial
        L-type
          multi-function tool.

Rather than errand girl, don't I wish I were a worker
knowing how to wield sophisticated gizmos
to repair or build a building
where people like me are safe, pamper dogs,
read books, and think about the world.
When it comes to survival or self-sufficiency, I falter.
And suffer a bit of shame at being unhandy
at most things made by hand except a poem
constructed to be both sturdy and ephemeral.

Speaking of Dogs: a Poem Sequence

1.

The dog next door barks in the dawn,
insistent as a rooster.
It's a long slow dawn.
What does the dog want?
To go inside where humans stir?
Or is he angry at a squirrel
he can't catch in his pinpoint teeth?

My husband lies in bed
blocking the noise
with a ceiling of pillows over his face.
What does he want?
Sometimes I'm close and know;
other times I'm left outside, barking,
barking to be let in.

2.

At the corner, a man shovels out the hydrant
buried by a blizzard's wild fling.
The red cap of its top emerges followed by
a stout cylindrical body.

My neighbor says he unburies the post not
for fire disaster but to enable earnest tagging
by some dogs and the enlightenment of others
that stop to smell the daily news.

3.

My dog can't hold her pee.
When excited she sprinkles the floor.

A little boy at the baseball game
cried when he sotted his shorts.
His parents scolded him—
what are you, a baby?

Some teenage girls wet
their panties when they're tickled.

Women my age often
pass a little water as the saying goes,
when pollen counts go high
in heavy heat, and we sneeze.

I want someone to pat me
as I do my dog, and say
it's OK, old gal,
it happens to the best of us.

4.

My old dog scratches on the back door.
She carries indoors the outdoor smell of spring

and damp doggy hair. Her muzzle is white,
her hips bony like a dairy cow's.

She lets me pick up and wipe her paws
one at a time; as a tripod, she's wobbly.

After licking my ear to taste me, she slumps
on her rump awaiting my next move.

I want to be worthy, but no matter—
I'm a deity in her eyes.

Grove

If an aspen grove begins to grow
by your house you will not be sorry

to dwell near an ancient being
older than sequoias.

From a single seed
at the end of an ice age,

aspen shoots became trees
rooted underground, all one,

as you and everyone
you've loved, everything touched,

heard, lost and found again forms
something like a grove.

Place one leaf under your tongue
to speak with eloquence.

If you are afraid, be soothed
by elixir extracted from bark.

Someday a stranger may come
to your door, ask to sit in aspen shade

hearing old voices and new
vibrate through the golden leaves.

Godspeed

Doesn't everything die at last, and too soon?
– Mary Oliver

1.

I'm thinking of you, sister,
world traveler, artist, mother,
during my plane's uneasy climb
up a dark stairway of clouds.
I'm coming for your leave-taking
or to touch your abandoned body.
Don't wait until I arrive.
Let go of beauty and troubles.
Life insists on death.

Recalling magnificent paintings
of heaven makes me imagine
you experiencing radiance
above cloudbanks.
It's not much farther now
to breaking through the scrim
dividing what we understand
from a blind at the center
of all we don't know.

2.

My sister's body is restless
awaiting its death.
Her porcelain face on the big pillow
looks like our mother's on her last day.
Family and friends

hold her hand, lean over the bed
to whisper.

At the edges of the hospital room
shadows pool like dark water.
We want to open
locked windows to birdsong.

3.

River, tell me, as your current
dispatches a handful of ashes
to the sea, when you take
the gray dust of her
into water and deliver it
at journey's end,
does her spirit hover
like a butterfly
over cosmos in golden bloom?
River, trembling traveler, what
do you carry of her from one place
to the next—stories? An uncle's love?
A bright color she wore?
Will the ocean welcome everything
into its salty realm?

Winter on the Farm

Cows plodded from frozen fields
to be shuttered in the barn
and milked in the cold,
their damp breath forming clouds.
All at once dark enclosed everything
in the hard hold of winter
as if snow with its quilted silence
would fall forever on fence posts
and garlands of barbed wire.

My grandparents lived in tremulous times,
their farm work hard as December dirt.
They could not hibernate from duty,
could not retreat and be sustained
only by prayer, but had to coax life
from a narrow gap the way
they guided a calf out of its mother,
bloodied, bleating, eyes open wide.

White Horse

As a winter girl I'd wake in the dark,
dress in a hooded parka for chores,
plod through snow to the barn
where it smelled of alfalfa and sour dung.
Cold pounded my bones.

In their slight shanties
how did Dakota homesteaders endure?
Many did not.
Remember Beret who went mad.

Sometimes frantic scuttle of claws
on metal would say a mouse
had fallen into the feed bin,
trapped by its own hunger.

Blinking in the flashlight's beam
the white horse lay folded on straw
where she slept through
the boredom of long nights.

I watched her rise, front legs pulling
her torso and back legs from the floor
as if climbing from a pit
to stand sixteen hands high.

Bulked up with inactivity
and a thick coat she lumbered
to the field to shake,
her breath quick and cloudy.
One time in a snow flurry,

she turned sharply and galloped away,
vanishing into a whiteout
as if ridden by a thief.

I wanted to shout: *Take me, too.*

Fed by United Farm Workers

First day of college
I met the avocado
at a common table
laden with unfamiliar fruits
or were they vegetables?

A foreigner from the North
I traveled knowing little
about the warm country.
Tray in hand,
a local girl from my dorm
brought me to a line
of cosmic eaters—
boys in Sly Stone T-shirts,
girls in flip-flops.

My sleek California guide
from the foothills
near campus
showed me a thing
or three at lunch.
I put on my plate
what she pointed to:
a fresh fig rich
as fall heat.
A fanged artichoke
with its soft heart.
An avocado to strip
of its nubby skin,
remove its stone belly,

cut into creamy pieces
two-toned green.

Who gave these jewels
to us, I didn't think
to question.
And why no grapes?
I didn't know field workers
were meagerly paid
for growing food
they couldn't afford to eat.
Viva La Causa!
I would learn to shout,
but not yet.

Gather the Wind

Papa kept his head down,
jaw squared to the world.
Mama buttoned up her joy
like an old-fashioned blouse
to please Papa when the time came.
Muddy Mo was Papa's river.
Sweet yellow clover, Mama's flower.

Mama let us girls run wild
in winds that herded clouds
like horses from prairies
beyond the skyline.
Papa's mostly absent
from the family's velvet album;
he kept the camera eye on us.

He dwelled in fierce silence.
She had a song for every occasion:
church, sleepless child, chores
that took her to her knees.
He did the math; she wrote
letters and sent newspaper clips
to daughters when we left.

Mama, I want to come back now
I'm old and done with busy places.
A windbreak shelters the house
with its white clapboard and lilac bush.
Papa, I ask you what star to follow

and when I lie down, will the wind
still and let me sleep?

after Joni Mitchell's "Let the Wind Carry Me"

Snow Angels and William Blake

I used to fall backward on purpose
into snow's clean cold sheets.
My mother would pull me up to leave
a crisp image of a snow angel behind,
blue shadows filling the wings.

In the kitchen, my mother wore
an apron embroidered with stars.
She called the early dark a shawl
for the house to wear.

Some say William Blake was mad,
simple like a child, or brilliant
who saw the body of his brother after death
ascending as an angel
laughing with joy.
A cold season isn't simple.

Mostly we stay inside with sober thoughts.
Animals grow thick or thin and hide.
Through the lengthening nights
we wish for safe passage
and a visitation of fresh snow.

Spirited Away

After my mother's death I never knew
when the bully of a big sob
would punch its way out of my chest.
I avoided parties, cut my long hair short,
lost weight. Blood forgot
its monthly flow as I grew smaller
as if to fit into childhood's arms, go back
into her body, begin again
to be loved by her.

Feral grief made me exit a college course
in the middle of a sentence I could not finish.
I climbed down a steep path to stare
at the river unrolling its steel ribbon
under a bridge where John Berryman jumped.

From above, a voice shouted *Don't move.*
I shook my head *no.* A boy elfin as Peter Pan
clambered down from a ledge
to sit with me, watchful and quiet.
I showed him what it looked like
to weep your heart out.

When I could stand, when I could leave
to rejoin to my life, I looked back—
the boy and the terrible greed.
of my grief had disappeared.

The Ring Video Doorbell Bares Trouble

Trouble
comes in plain daylight, and trouble
comes in night's tunnel, our untethered son's troubles
visible on his bleary face that we view as a troubled
image on our phone; he's just outside the door—troubling
us to decide whether it's safe to let him in, since trouble
shadows him, sometimes car trouble,
other times when he's wild, it's booze trouble
or money, mood or drug trouble.
He's mumbling *let me in it's cold out here.* A troubled
debate happens in our bedroom, me saying troubled
sleep is not good for us, and my husband's troubled
words whispering: *what's more troubling—*
him sleeping it off on the sofa or letting more trouble
stalk him as he stumbles toward god knows what double trouble
at 2 a.m. He's a brown man on foot in a city troubled
by recent deaths at the hands of men in blue; what is life for
but to trouble
oneself to care for loved ones in good times and
through their troubles.

A Memory of the Seventh Day

wth heavy snow,
when the storm rested like Yahweh
satisfied with a cold white heaven,

my son, dribbling a manna of milk from
his cereal bowl, pointed with his spoon
at snowy shapes on branches: "Look! Angels!"

My husband's relatives praise God,
believe they have reservations
in a paradise that might look like today.

My mother-in-law's faith assured her
she'd be dressed in flesh after death,
whole again, her missing breast back.

I paused for what could have been
an eternity that morning in the kitchen,
clock stilled, my happy child nearby

who stared outside, expecting another
arrival of angels, and in the meantime,
asked for more Cheerios.

Internet Impulse Error

Whoosh, bagged and gone, that hour
of anguish spent searching Facebook
for a posting you want to take down,
remove, stop its seep and spread.

Beware twitchy fingers and a blear moment
when you experience a blaze
of ultra-therapeutic and inappropriate sharing
with the whole wide world of net.

You aren't a red-lipped actress
with a not-so-secret lover or a goon squad
evangelist that people want to follow,
so perhaps your misstep will not be liked,
shared, emojied with frowns and worse.

Chances are this malodorous remark
affiliated with your name will someday rise
from the demented foreverness
of social media and wave a red flag
provoking herd instinct of sharp-horned
shamers to stampede and gore.

You might as well sell your house,
downsize and move to Little Diomede,
a remote dot in the Bering Strait
where you'll never learn
whether you've been outed
and where a simply lovely life
can be lived anonymously.

Rant: Bad Day with Diamonds and Toads

A fierce storm's diamond opulence
suggests global warming.
Ice teeth grow pointy
on the eaves of my house.
I aspire and fail to be unhaunted
by angers, ice dams and guilt.
I belong to the fat crowd
responsible for the floods.

In one brief morning, I annoyed
three people; two fought back
making daylight darken.
Words I spat would have been
washed out with soap in the long ago.
A gaping hole in the roof
makes me curse, too agitated
to make amends, ashamed to be
the foul sister in a fairy tale
whose mouth spewed
coal lumps and toads.

I repeat the serenity prayer
and *ah-uu-mm* syllables
like warm honey on sticky wounds
until fierce buzzing
in my frontal lobe disappears
like a hive of absconding bees.

The Way to Cold Mountain

Walk up the valley from a dynasty
of despair, through the fog, into the air
of high mountains sweet with solitude.
Trails braid together into one pigtail.
Follow.

Here no one points the snout
of a gun in your face.

Any child on your back is alive
and not too heavy to carry.

If you want to be known,
turn back to cities
with their heroes-of-war statues,
to vast colonies where people work
by rote as ants or ruffians
disrupting the harmony of common good.

Do not be insect or lout.
Make by hand the gifts you bring,
otherwise the wind might cry thief! thief!

Stop at the place where the compass
of your heart stops spinning.

When you get there, don't be foolish
expecting the bright bird you carried
in a cage to sing in captivity.

Let it loose!

Come to Cold Mountain
undated, undetected, humble
and smooth as the egg of creation.

Into the Garden Come

Wander with her not lonely as a cloud but purposeful through
acres of plants with thousands of jutting green stems
and branches geysering from hundreds of pots, each tagged
with a price and a come-hither-and-take-me-home name
like Holy Grail hibiscus and Wildberry coral bells.
She's out to exchange cash for bluestone cobbles
and flowering perennials that will please the bees and her
with extra blooms to vase.

She studies and notes, composes and works the soil. Her Eden
not only improves, but also fails, which is like human life
rising and falling, so this: while the pink anemones prosper,
the Japanese grass wilts. When the dogwood wears its rouge
and thrives, the false Solomon seal crisps and dies. If she
could bring spring back to her body, she'd be a slim blade
of Soft Winds iris, her hair the color of red sunflowers,
and on her hands, two thoroughly green thumbs.

Each April inflates hope as she redesigns the garden, buys,
transplants, renews, divides, expands, clips, fertilizes, tests
and dreams. One spring she realizes how many years
she's gardened by the height of a crabapple tree planted
as a young shoot that now grazes electric wires. Her face
is more full of folds and wrinkles than the tree's trunk.
When her house and yard pass on to new owners,
she wants them to recognize that this little land was loved—
each unfurled bud, each beetle and earthworm—and that
the gardener was buried with dirt under her nails.

title adapted from an Emily Dickinson poem

Banana, Sunrise, Chair

1.

A question lobbed at me
while watching a tournament on TV:
Who's your all-time favorite tennis player?

I couldn't recall her name.

It took an hour picturing a woman
carried into a stadium
50 years ago on a golden throne
before I found a distant drawer
in my brain and announced:
Billy Jean King!

2.

For a memory test the nurse says
three words, then reviews meds,
asks if I'm safe at home,
asks if rugs I could trip on
have been removed.
After what seems like an hour
of games, she springs a pop quiz:
can I recall the three words?

Like a good student, I recite
banana, sunrise, chair.
I haven't yet lost
all my marbles.

Snowbirds

For those of us escaping ice
that lurks slippery under snow
it's an Eden. In Arizona
honied daylight glows, yellow
flowers bloom. We wear clothes
weighing next to nothing. We used
to work all the time. Now
older Americans in the 21th Century
don't have jobs, but still get paid
to live and travel, buy books and food.

As it does elsewhere, a serpent hisses.
In this particular paradise, thorns stab skin
like fishhooks. The Colorado River
has been sliced into so many rivulets
and sold. Water tables near Tucson
lower. Here come more thirsty visitors:
northerners for warmth and pleasure,
migrants from the south for safety and work.

After dark, temperatures drop. People
need coats and wool shawls to survive
the desert. What knows nights' bitter
cold? Rattlesnakes know.
Spanish-whispering people know.

Triolet for My Sister a Year After Cremation

To secure bloom again the season she was born
a cup of bonemeal was fed the yellow rose.
On a bench, green gloves she's always worn
to tend bloom in spring when she was born
and to shield her soft hands, rest forlorn.
A life of growth and harvest dying doesn't close.
Come see her blooming the season she was born.
Bonemeal of her ashes begets a yellow rose.

Postcard from Oakland

An open-air café atop a tall hotel
offers a view of San Francisco
in evening clothes of bay blue.
To the west, dark overtakes
tangerine clouds while millions
of lights begin to glint.

It's a lucky life to be surveying
such a scene of black and sparkle,
no ominous smoke from fires,
no danger of Qassam rockets,
no drones foraging like giant bats.

We drink clean water, afford food,
sleep well in houses under the same
moon as Palestine, as Israel, a blood
moon that climbs its hidden trellis
like one of the pale roses
still in bloom by Lake Merritt,
so tender it will not survive the night.

When Rain Comes

the roof lets it descend whether
in hard bursts or gentle
strokes that wet the temples
of pine where sparrows bide.
You can't give it an ultimatum.
It arrives inevitably as night
with its long thoughts.

In the age of our failure—
we parents whose legacy
is adages, antique furniture
and protests against war—
our children eye the future
like marksmen. At the table
they look at anything but us.

In a time of change (and when
isn't it?), you make slow broth,
recall practice required
to play "Clair de Lune."
You have stood too long. Sit down.

Rain, wash the little faces
of red berries hardened
after the crabapple bloomed.
Melancholy moves
like a weather front
that will not stay forever.

Gift from the Sea by Anne Morrow Lindbergh

Beloved book of my landlocked mother
I drew from my bookshelf today
to read and borrow from Anne
who learned from saints' language
of longing to live in grace.

Like Anne, like my mother,
I'm a woman busy with life's
errands, dust, and caring—
no time to hermit like Saint John
who followed a light
or to walk El Camino de Santiago
as a pilgrim.

For a brief rest I robe
in loose cotton clothes,
sit outside in leaf filtered shade.
After a chapter of reading,
I lay the book in my lap.
Silence amplifies the holy present
sound of birds' whirl, lisp
of dry grass, and breathing
like tides of a sea.

Index

Acknowledgments

MARGARET IS GRATEFUL to publisher Norton Stillman of Nodin Press for giving her poems a home, and for a friendship that has grown over the years. They refer to their friendship as "between," borrowing the term philosopher Martin Buber used for the nature of all relations.

John Toren, who helped edit and design almost all of Margaret's books, has done so with smarts, skill, and goodwill.

Warm thanks to Donna Isaac, David Grothe, Joan Johnson, Angie Kirby, Carol Masters, Patsy Noble, Suki Sun and Connie Wanek who helped select poems for this book. A special nod goes to Joan who first suggested the title, *Belongings*.

Emily Dickinson wrote of "her divine majority." Comprising Margaret's divine majority are her parents, siblings, husband David Grothe, son Michael Grothe, his wife Claire Dunlap, son Alex Grothe, and beloved friends who know who they are.

Poets too numerous to name, from present and past times, some near and known personally, others encountered through their poetry, have deepened Margaret's appreciation of writing and of life.

Twelve poems from *In a Sheep's Eye, Darling*, copyright © 1988 by Margaret Hasse, are reprinted with the permission of The Permissions Company, LLC on behalf of Milkweed Editions, milkweed.org., all rights reserved. Poems from *The Call of Glacier Park* reprinted by permission of Finishing Line Press. Thanks to New Rivers Press for the first release of *Stars Above, Stars Below*. In 2018 Nodin Press acquired the book and reissued it. All other books from which poems are selected were published by Nodin Press.

The author wishes to thank the following publications and places that have featured her poems over the years—so many years that some of these journals have passed, and others may have been unwittingly left off the list.

A Change in Weather: Midwest Women Poets • *A Little Book of Abundance* • *A Pause for Beauty: The Heron Dance* • *A View from The Loft* • *Bearings Online* • *Beloved on the Earth: Poems of Grief and Gratitude* • *Broad Wings, Long Legs: A Rookery of Heron Poems* • *Bryant Literary Review* • *Boomer Lit Magazine* • *Border Crossings* • *Calyx: A Journal of Art and Literature by Women* • *Common Good Books bookstore website* • *County Lines* • *Dacotah Territory* • *Eating the Pure Light: Homage to Tom McGrath* • *Flurry* • *Fresh Air (a magazine of KFAI Radio)* • *Great River Review* • *Healing the Divide: Poems of Kindness and Connection* • *Horizons: The South Dakota Writers' Anthology* • *Ice Cream Poems: World Enough Writers* • *Iowa Environmental Council Newsletter* • *Low Down and Coming On: A Feast of Delicious and Dangerous Poems about Pigs* • *MidAmerican Review* • *Milkweed Chronicle* • *Minnesota Conservation Volunteer* • *Minnesota Monthly* • *Minnesota Poetry Calendar 2000* • *Miramar* • *Moons and Lions Tailes (sic)* • *Northeast* • *Northern Lit Quarterly* • *Persimmon Tree* • *Poet Lore* • *Poetry City U.S.A.* • *Poetry Foundation* • *Poetry East* • *Quiddity* • *Rag Queen Periodical* • *Rewilding Hope* • *River Images* • *Sister Black Bike Press* • *Sisters of the Earth: Women's Prose and Poetry about Nature* • *Sleet Magazine* • *Soundings: Door County in Poetry* • *South*

Dakota Review • *Saint Paul Almanac* • *Soundings: Door County in Poetry* • *Sunbury* • *Surprised by Joy: a Wising Up Anthology* • *Talking Stick* • *The Great Circumpolar Bear Cult* • *The Heart of All That Is: Reflections on Home* • *The Kindness of Strangers: A Wising Up Anthology* • *The Lake Street Review* • *The Midwest Quarterly* • *The Moccasin* • *The Nations Underground: Writing With Our Ancestors* • *The Path to Kindness: Poems of Connection and Joy* • *The Sun* • *The Talking of Hands* • *The Wind Blows, the Ice Breaks: Poems of Loss and Renewal* • *The Wonder of Small Things: Poems of Peace and Renewal* • *The Writers Almanac* • *Tinderbox* • *Touched by Adoption* • *Visiting Bob: Poems Inspired by the Life and Work of Bob Dylan* • *Verse-Virtual* • *WARM Journal* • *Water~Stone Review* • *What Light!* • *When One Voice Ends, Another Begins: 150 Years of Minnesota Poetry* • *Whistling Shade* • *Women's Lives, Women's Legacies* • *33 Minnesota Poets #2* • *142 Ways to Make a Poem*

Valuable institutional support for Margaret's life in poetry came from the Jerome Foundation, the Loft Literary Center and its Mentor Program and Loft-McKnight Awards, the Minnesota State Arts Board's Artists Fellowships with appropriations from the Minnesota State Legislature, the National Endowment for the Arts Creative Writing Fellowship, and the National Endowment for the Humanities' Voices & Visions project. Residencies at Anderson Center at Tower View, Norcroft Retreat for Women, Ragdale, and Write On, Door County provided quiet harbor for writing and fellowship with other writers. The University of Minnesota's Upper Midwest Literary Archives houses Margaret's papers.

About the Author

MARGARET HASSE began reading and writing poetry as a child and never stopped. She grew up in South Dakota and attended college in California where she earned a B.A. in English from Stanford University. After moving to Minnesota in 1973 she became deeply involved in its rapidly growing literary community. Over the years Margaret taught writing in correctional facilities, at The Loft Literary Center, for COMPAS Poets-in-the-Schools, as a freelancer, among other places. Alongside writing and teaching poetry Margaret worked for and as an adviser to arts organizations in the state and nationally. She also obtained an M.A. in English (with a creative writing emphasis) from the University of Minnesota.

Margaret's poetry has been widely published, including in six full-length books, two chapbooks, a "new and selected" collection, and in journals, anthologies, and, remarkably, in St. Paul's sidewalks and on public transit. Her work as a poet has received recognition through a National Endowment for the Arts fellowship, Loft McKnight Awards, Minnesota State Arts Board grants, and other honors. Margaret has lived in St. Paul for almost forty years with her husband, David Grothe, where they raised their two sons, Michael and Alex. To learn more, visit: margarethasse.com or https://www.poetryfoundation.org/poets/margaret-hasse